The Biblical Theme
in Modern Drama

THE BIBLICAL THEME
IN MODERN DRAMA

Marie Philomene de los Reyes, SPC

University of the Philippines Press
Quezon City, Philippines
1978

To Father
who would have rejoiced
to see this volume

Preface

When the present volume was submitted as a doctoral dissertation to the Sophia University of Tokyo in 1977, the panel that had studied it remarked:

> Biblical themes have inspired dramatic performances from the Middle Ages to the Baroque period. The subject was suppressed by the Protestant Reformers or went out of fashion in the Enlightenment. The reappearance of the theme in modern drama is a subject of great interest which so far has not found adequate treatment. The present study, therefore, fills a conspicuous gap.

My attention was first drawn to biblical themes in the drama of our century on reading plays like Christopher Fry's *The Firstborn* (1948), Archibald MacLeish's *J. B.* (1956), and Paul Claudel's *L'Annonce Faite à Marie* (1948). From the very start, therefore, I noticed that the resurgence of the biblical theme in drama was not limited to any one nation. The first step in the preparation of this book thus consisted in a verification of this resurgence: Did it really exist? The search made through histories of drama led to encounter with the twelve plays by the nine noteworthy dramatists studied in this work.

The twelve years that elapsed since research was started in 1965 were devoted not only to understanding these plays and dramatists, but also to an attempt to grasp the history of Western drama and theories of the same. During the course of the study, it has been fascinating to discover that what T.S. Eliot, the great literary giant of our century, once wrote by way of prophecy regarding the mythical method was actually being fulfilled by the dramatists of our century in their use of biblical themes.

The delight in discovery was not to be mine alone, for during the oral defense of the dissertation, one of those present made the comment that this research need not be considered as a completed study, but rather as a springboard for many other studies on a subject which is so rich, it is inexhaustible. Should this actually happen, the joy of the writer of this book would be multiplied.

To obtain access to material originally in German, I have been much indebted to Dr. Thomas Immoos of Sophia University, himself a linguist whose works on drama have been published in German, French and English. For advice and encouragement through the years, I should like to thank Dr. Joseph Roggendorf, Dr. Francis Mathy and Professors Motoshi Karita, Takero Oiji, Peter Milward and Donald Mason.

It is with pleasure, too, that I acknowledge the help of the Reverend Neal Henry Lawrence, OSB, and Sister Kathleen England, OSU, for reading the dissertation and giving invaluable suggestions.

Finally, I should like to express heartfelt thanks to the editorial staff of the University of the Philippines Press for assistance in seeing the book through its various publishing stages. To the members of the U.P. Press Board of Management who decided to accept this book for publication, the appreciation of a wandering Filipino.

MARIE PHILOMÈNE DE LOS REYES, SPC

August 15, 1978
Tokyo, Japan

Contents

Chapter

The Biblical Theme
in Modern Drama

CHAPTER ONE

The Resurgence of the Biblical Theme in Modern Drama

It is a truism to say that in Greece, as in Western Europe, drama had its cradle in religious cult. Just as Greek drama emerged from the choral expression of worship around the altar, so in the Christian nations, the mystery plays were nourished in the liturgy taking place in cathedrals, enacted by clerics themselves, until the guilds took over, and scriptural drama went out to the towns in the form of cycles. As long as the audiences were not yet well acquainted with the biblical narrative, its literal dramatization could very well satisfy them. However, a natural development of mystery plays took place in the humanized portrayal of scriptural figures, so that gradually, their "haloes" became dimmer, at times disappearing in the realistic presentation of characters and events.

The realism inherent in the process of humanization of scriptural drama could be felt in the humor which had the advantage of maintaining the attention of audiences already acquainted with the biblical story. Gradually, the scriptural scenes were enacted so realistically that even without legislation, dramatists themselves instinctively felt that God could no longer appear on the stage.[1] And the next step in the development was to keep Christ from the cast, presenting only peripheral figures of the New Testament such as John the Baptist, the prodigal son, etc. Still later on, even the Old Testament figures became difficult to present, and dramatists stepped down a lower rung to Apocrypha, then to subject matter taken from the history of Josephus,

---

[1] Murray Roston, *Biblical Drama in England* (London: Faber and Faber, 1968), p. 115.

satisfying themselves with the biblical setting, so as to be free from
the responsibility of using quotations from Holy Scripture.

This situation in biblical drama, along with the growing disrepute
of theatres in England toward the end of the sixteenth century onward
to the seventeenth, made people shrink from associating Holy Scripture
with the stage, both amateur and professional. Although the prohibition of the performance of scriptural plays was not legalized in written
form in England, the decision of the Examiner of Plays was tantamount
to law. Now, it is evident that scriptural drama disappeared from the
English stage for three centuries. According to Murray Roston:[2]

> Apart from one vague reference to the granting in 1662 of a licence
> 'to George Bayley, of London, musitioner, to make a show of a play
> called Noah's Flood' (which appears to have been some sort of musical
> presentation and hence not a biblical dramatization in the fullest sense),
> there is no record of any stage performance of biblical drama until a
> further dubious reference in 1793.

There was of course William II's ban to scenes "contrary to Religion
and good manners," but this was only concerned with "religious
indiscretions," not against biblical drama, for it did not exist on the
stage at the time. Roston concludes that the absence of scriptural
drama on the stage during this period was due less to legal prohibition
than to a tacit assumption that the dramatization of scriptural themes
was in some sense profane.[3]

In France, the staging of mystery plays was banned in Paris as
early as November 17, 1548.[4] Although the prohibition was issued
only in one city and for one company of actors, *les confrères de la
Passion*, Petit de Julleville declares that it was Paris that decided the
fashion for the whole France: "What died out in Paris would soon
languish in all the provinces."[5]

Several causes are mentioned as leading to the disappearance of
mystery plays from the stage in France: the attacks of Protestants,
the scruples of Catholics and the disgust of men of letters with the
poor taste of the language in which many of the popular religious
plays were being written.[6] What the Protestants objected to was the

---

[2] *Ibid.*, p. 179.
[3] *Ibid.*, p. 180.
[4] Petit de Julleville, *Le Théâtre en France* (Paris: Librarie Armand Colin,
1923), p. 71.
[5] *Ibid.*, p. 72.
[6] *Ibid.*

"audacious licence" with which parts of the Bible were being staged, in an endless admixture of the ornamental and the fictitious, in comic episodes designed for pleasantry, in such a way as to alter the tone of the Scriptures. The Catholics, on the other hand, were soon led to suspect that too much intimacy in the presentation of the Bible (which had become the Protestants' symbol of revolt) could be a snare to the weak in faith.[7] The attitude of men of letters is reflected by Jean de la Taille who, in his work, *L'Art de la Tragédie* (1572), expressed the wish that what he called "the bitter spices" which corrupt the savour of the French tongue should be exterminated in the country, so that instead of the old plays catering to the popular taste, the true tragedy and comedy should be adopted.[8]

The Paris prohibition against the staging of mystery plays, however, could not prevent altogether the writing of biblical tragedies. The elimination of the comic element, the sustained seriousness of style followed could calm down scruples. Thus, as early as three years after the prohibition, Theodore de Beze's play entitled *Abraham Sacrifiant* was produced at Lausanne; three decades later (1580), Thomas Lecocq's tragedy, *Cain*, was performed, borrowing much from the old theatre of mystery plays while paying attention to the trimming of style.[9]

Reverence of Holy Scripture was therefore a feeling shared by the French. Yet, it did not seem so relentless as that of the English who virtually banned the performance of scriptural dramas on the professional stage for three centuries. When Oscar Wilde wrote *Salome* (1895), it was in French simply because it could not be performed on the English stage due to its biblical theme. It was produced in Paris in 1898.

Despite this ban on the staging of biblical drama, the urge to dramatize the scriptural narrative must have been great, for the English tried to get around the prohibition in at least two ways. The first of these is the invention of the oratorio as a means for reviving scriptural drama. The German-born British composer, George Frederick Handel (1685–1759), found a way of combining dramatization of a biblical theme with the inspiring solemnity of church music, so that the figures,

---

[7] *Ibid.*
[8] *Ibid.*, p. 73.
[9] *Ibid.*, pp. 83-84.

so to speak, remain "haloed" and are kept at respectful distance. It is certain that the device of setting biblical drama to solemn music prevented the development of complete realism; the unrealistic style of performance was necessary during this period in order to permit the dramatization of the Bible. The scriptural oratorio, which has become a cherished part of the English heritage, is indeed an attempt to edge biblical drama onto the English stage under cover of its musical accompaniment.[10] Thus, thousands flocked to the performance of Handel's scriptural oratorios, among which we have *Messiah*, that triumphant work of art. Through the years, audiences went to listen to the music that Handel had composed for *Esther, Deborah, Athalia, Saul, Israel in Egypt, Samson, Belshazzar, Judas Maccabaeus, Joshua, Solomon, Susanna* and *Jephtha*.

The other outlets for the urge to dramatize Holy Scripture were the numerous closet dramas written by a legion of writers, mostly dramatists whose names are unfamiliar, except Byron's and Elizabeth Barrett Browning's. If it was beyond the dramatist's aspirations to write for audiences, then at least, he could write for the readers who would not be prohibited from satisfying their devotion by reading dramatized versions of the Bible.

To one ignorant of the reasons for the disappearance of biblical dramas during the last three centuries, it is easy to make the specious statement attributing the phenomenon to the attacks against the sacred made during the period of the Enlightenment. It seems to me, however, that the influence of the antireligious spirit born of rationalism was felt much later. In fact, the spirit of the Enlightenment made its full impact on biblical drama precisely during the beginning of the re-surgence of biblical themes being studied in this volume. For, if as considered in the preceding pages, the dramatists were banned from staging biblical plays because of a sense of reverence that would protect Holy Scripture from association with such a profane place as the theatre, then the impulse of rationalism would be the opposite. Why, the rationalist could ask, should biblical subject matter be taboo on the stage? Are not scriptural figures men of flesh and blood like us? Denying the possibility of miracles, the rationalist attitude would be to expose them to ridicule. Such iconoclasm was actually the swinging of the pendulum to the opposite direction in the realm of biblical

---

10 Murray Roston, *op. cit.,* p. 183.

drama. Where the Puritanic tendency had been to refrain from presenting scriptural figures on the stage for fear of sacrilege, the rationalist could present these same heroes stripped of their haloes. The new trend "to reassess the biblical narrative by discounting the miracles, and visualizing the biblical figures in entirely human terms," made iconoclasts start tearing down the scriptural heroes from their pedestals, presenting the innocent as villains, and acquitting the guilty. Such, for instance, were D.H. Lawrence's *The Man Who Died* (1931) with its suggestion that Christ could indulge in carnal love; Arnold Bennett's *Judith* (1918) in which the heroine is so portrayed as to make *The Times* complain that "although her lascivious advances to Holofernes must be accepted as justified by the original text, her immodest behaviour to others was indefensible." She is presented as ogling the Governor, ogling a young captive whom she ultimately marries. John Masefield, in *A King's Daughter* (1923), "applying to the theme the new conception of the Old Testament as a series of pharisaically biased accounts, transposed the virtuous and the guilty to reveal the supposed truth concealed by the historian's prejudice."[11] Thus, Jezebel is portrayed as the loyal wife who believes in the purity of her inherited religion, struggling to establish justice and peace among her subjects, while Naboth is transformed into a coarse, stubborn braggart who answers her gentle reasoning with a stream of insults, so that the righteous cause is no longer Naboth's but Jezebel's. According to Roston, this is an arbitrary rewriting of the story with the express purpose of whitewashing the villains and blackening the heroes—a form of deliberate iconoclasm rather than the pursuit of truth.[12]

The orthodox are amply justified in fearing that such freedom in the handling of biblical themes on the stage would lead to "flagrant heresy," yet this same freedom was not altogether without its advantages. It enabled biblical drama to move from its "closet" existence to the fresh air of professional performance in the theatre, freeing the portrayal of scriptural figures from excessive artificialization which had been a barrier to their humanization.

Even within the very period of resurgence, the pendulum was already swinging to the opposite direction. When the dramatists had

---

11 *Ibid.*, p. 248.
12 *Ibid.*, p. 249.

spent their force painting the scriptural heroes black and whitewashing the villains, a greater seriousness in appraisal was once more creeping into biblical drama, a quality felt even in its very humor. Instrumental in bringing about this change in England was the Religious Drama Society whose invitation for the writing of religious plays was answered by giant figures like Christopher Fry and T.S. Eliot. *Murder in the Cathedral* was first performed at Canterbury in 1935, and Christopher Fry's first religious play, *The Boy with a Cart* (1939), was written within this movement.

By then, however, the biblical theme had undergone such transformation in its dramatic presentation that it is difficult to recognize it as identical to the motifs that had given form to the first mystery plays of Europe. The resurgence being considered in this study is not just a revival of old mystery plays; it is rather the emergence of a new creative energy in the presentation of biblical themes, affecting the very structure of drama in modern times. For the biblical theme had never really died in European drama, but its use had become lifeless, choked with the inhibitions that came with the prohibition of its professional performance. What was needed was a new impetus, and this we have had full grown in our century.

In the study of modern drama, we must go back to Henrik Ibsen whose plays mark a turning point, both in subject matter and in technique. His presentation of "the women question" in *A Doll's House* (1879) is said to have "shocked the sentimental optimists who want a happy ending to all human questions on the stage."[13] In technique, the play shows Ibsen's indebtedness to Scribe and the French dramatists, for up to the obligatory scene when Helmer and Nora face each other, *A Doll's House* shows the characteristics of the well-made play. But at this crucial moment, the tragedy of Nora as a woman decidedly overshadows the dramatic plot. The last scene of the play, by the very storm of protest which it aroused, proves the impact which Ibsen has had on the world of theatre.

What Ibsen inaugurated was but a period of transition in which modern drama was to struggle for recognition. After Ibsen, the old theory of drama as defined by Aristotle and his followers, and systematized by Scribe and the French dramatists, would be challenged by

---

[13] Donald Clive Stuart, *The Development of Dramatic Art* (New York: Dover Publications, Inc., 1960), p. 576.

the practice of dramatists from various countries. Aristotle had claimed that the essence of drama was action; the static and mood dramas of Chekhov and Maeterlinck would pit themselves against this notion. Chekhov's ideals as a dramatist have been summed up as a freeing of the stage from routine and stereotypes, to seek theatricality of dramatic production not in exceptional staging but in hidden inner psychologic life.[14] This he effected not only by the words he gives his characters to speak, but also in the pauses of their dialogue and in the words they leave unspoken. Beyond what appears on the stage is the real human life; beyond what the characters do and say is the real human being: "a complex tissue of thoughts, dreams and moods, sensations, emotions, which he is incapable of analyzing." In the Chekhovian play we feel a mystic emotion which is very real, but we find it difficult to analyze the plot and characters in words.

Maeterlinck, like Chekhov, found the true tragic element in life, not in the material and psychological struggle of people, but in their moments of tranquility and silence. Sound, silence, light and color, together with the obscure implications of the spoken words: these are the most important elements of Maeterlinck's symbolism and dramatic effects. With these, he is capable of evoking "the invisible, the intangible, the subconscious and the unintelligible." This is what Sarcey has called with some contempt, the Maeterlinckian beyond: the invisible place which is just beyond the visible scene of action.[15] Thus, in Chekhov and in Maeterlinck, the old notion of the essence of drama as action has been challenged. There is a dream in their plays which cannot be explained.

One more major dramatist entered the Maeterlinckian dream world: Strindberg, in his trilogy, *To Damascus*. However, his contribution to the progress of modern drama as a challenge to the old, lay in another direction. There is, in Strindberg's monodramas, a dissent from the theory of drama as essentially action in which conflicting forces clash, whether as opposing individuals or groups. Strindberg's characters are "concepts of all the elements and influences which form the human soul. His people are never fixed. They are changing organisms."[16] Hence, Strindberg's hero, instead of clashing with an

---

14 *Ibid.*, p. 606.
15 *Ibid.*, p. 631.
16 *Ibid.*, p. 639.

antagonist, subdivides, meeting himself, so to speak, in different phases of his own entity, so that the other characters are but various expressions of himself. In his prefatory note to *The Dream Play*, he writes:[17]

> As he did in his previous dream play (*To Damascus*), so in this one the author has tried to imitate the disconnected but seemingly logical form of the dream. Anything may happen; everything is possible and probable. Time and space do not exist. On an insignificant background of reality, imagination designs and embroiders novel patterns, free fancies, absurdities and improvisations.
>
> The characters split, double, multiply, vanish, solidify, blur, clarify. But one consciousness reigns above them all—that of the dreamer; and before it there are no secrets, no incongruities, no scruples, no laws.

Thus, with the nourishing of the intangible which defies reason, the deintellectualization sown by Ibsen seems capable of sprouting in an almost infinite variety of ways, whether it be in Russian, in French or in Swedish.

It is significant, however, that when Ibsen was hailed by the Germans as "the regenerator of dramatic art," he remarked: "They had long had their Hebbel." With the rise of realism in Germany, we find Hebbel reverting to the biblical theme. In his works we notice the curious mixture of old dramaturgy and new, for in *Judith* (1840) and in *Herodes und Mariamne* (1850), he makes use of the historical presentation which had been employed for biblical material in drama since the time of the mystery plays. But in *Maria Magdalena* (1844), he follows an altogether new method, thus striking the note of modern dramaturgy in the treatment of the biblical theme. Hebbel's Maria Magdalena is no longer the sister of Lazarus and Martha leaving her home for a life of pleasure as we have her in the traditional interpretation of the biblical narrative. She is the daughter of a respectable middle-class home in a nineteenth-century German village, giving pain to her family through some sin of weakness. Now, this transposition of plot from the biblical narrative to a contemporary situation is one of the methods utilized in modern drama. If, therefore, Ibsen is considered the father of modern drama, in general, I think that the new

---

17 *Ibid.*, as quoted by D.C. Stuart.

impulse in the treatment of the biblical theme in modern drama, as studied in this thesis, can be traced to Hebbel.

It is difficult to seize on any particular year as marking the beginning of the triumph of modern drama, but studies on drama point to the year 1920 as a kind of dividing line between the new and the old in dramatic literature.[18] In France, Claudel and Cocteau were by then contributing their antinaturalistic pieces to the theatre. In England, the work of Bernard Shaw, who had been responsible for daring experiments on the stage, had begun to show a change "from naturalism to frank imaginative treatment."[19] Eugene O'Neill had reached Broadway by 1920, and with the publication of *The Emperor Jones*, he was well on the road mapped out by expressionism. As for Bertolt Brecht, he was at the time launching out on his career in the epic theatre which would become one of the most discussed of contemporary theories on drama.

That playwrights after the 1890s strove for innovation cannot be denied. Andre Barsacq, speaking of French postwar drama, declared that "The theatre is trying to throw off the restraints of the conventions in which it existed up to the war, and is, in consequence, enjoying more freedom in the construction of plays, and even in their subject matter."[20] Despite the opinion that avant-garde-ism in the theatre had taken place between 1880 and 1930, contemporary drama still exhibits the desire to be "new and daring, to be 'theatrical' in the theatre."

Among countless experiments in modern drama, I have selected from those written by dramatists of note after 1920, a number of plays in which I detected the biblical theme.[21] To think of theme wholly in the abstract would make the term all-inclusive; for what theme, in this sense, could be excluded from the Bible, whether it be of love or hate, good or evil, joy or sorrow, or whatever human values one might wish to consider. When I speak of biblical theme

---

[18] Cf. Allardyce Nicoll, *British Drama* (London: George G. Harrap, 1961), p. 456.

Cf. Bamber Gascoigne, *Twentieth Century Drama* (Hutchinson of London, 1962), pp. 7 ff.

[19] *Ibid.*, p. 457.

[20] In an interview in *Cambridge Opinion* 21, 1960. Quoted by Bamber Gascoigne, *op. cit.*, p. 9.

[21] Of the plays to be discussed, the first version of Claudel's *L'Annonce faite à Marie* was written in 1910. It went through a process of revision, however, and was given its final form only in 1948.

in this work, therefore, I refer to subject matter taken from the Bible: "plot containing already the elements of tension or causal connection before the process of literary fashioning has set in;"[22] the term has also been interpreted to include motif, as for instance, return from the dead (Lazarus theme), the innocent victim offering an oblation of suffering for redemptive aims (theme of redemption).

In the first group of plays being discussed, it will be difficult to discern the differences between the old dramaturgy and the new. Gradually, however, the new creative impulse will be seen to emerge more clearly, showing what a long way dramatists have trodden in the handling of the biblical theme since the period of the mystery plays in Europe.

Studying some of the works of representative playwrights of our century in England and America, as well as of three dramatists from France who can aid in illuminating the phenomenon, I should like to find out whether the resurgence of the biblical theme, in modern drama, aside from giving proof to varying attitudes of scriptural exegesis among playwrights, does point to any significant trend in the literature of our times.

---

22 Quoted from J. Roggendorf's review on Elizabeth Frenzel's *Stoffe der Weltliteratur,* in *Sophia* (Winter 1962), pp. 92-95.

CHAPTER TWO

Experiments with Biblical Themes

In exploring the potentialities of biblical materials, dramatists of our century have performed, so to speak, a wide range of experiments in accordance with varying creative compulsions and outlooks. Various movements of literature are perceivable in these dramatic creations. And in their attempt to integrate old materials into the new, or vice versa, dramatists have called to service some of the most recent scientific methods, the most subtle ideologies produced by the modern mind.

The audacities of these experiments can well be amazing. The biblical material is indubitably present, but the reaction to its use will vary from a shocked sensibility to a rapt wonderment at the evidence of either distortion or integration or transformation of biblical material, so as to present something comprehensible to the age, to produce some novelty out of the fusion of old materials with the new, or just to satisfy the inner impulse that prompted the dramatist to create his play.

RE-CREATION OF BIBLICAL CHARACTERS THROUGH PSYCHOLOGY

One of the modern sciences taken into the service of literature is psychology. Through its aid, many a writer today has succeeded in rendering old subjects ever more engrossing through the multicolored interpretations of the science. This is evident among dramatists who employ the biblical theme. It would seem as if psychology were the magic wand with which they summon figures from ancient times, making them tread the paths of our world once more, clad fascinatingly enough to captivate even the motley crowd of the theatre. Because psychology proposes to satisfy man's insatiable curiosity about himself and about the men and women he comes across in daily life, the psychological method is nearly always sure of gaining attention.

In the absence of a common faith which would be necessary for communion with their audiences, dramatists have sought the nearest substitute in the common interest in psychology. If theatre-goers today can no longer give full credence to the biblical narrative, let them at least recognize themselves and their own world in the personages and events presented in the Bible. The playwright who starts consciously or unconsciously with this premise in writing a play which draws material from the Scriptures, has the further advantage of being able to count at least on a knowledge of the Bible, if not always on its acceptance. For, sceptical though today's audience may be, its cultural background can still include an acquaintance with the biblical account. Hence, though a dramatist may choose to present a biblical theme in its historical setting, he can concentrate on the psychological truth of the characters, the thoughts and feelings which motivate them under certain circumstances.

In our study of the plays being discussed in this section, it would be pertinent to find out what role the dramatist assigns to psychology in his writing. Is he using psychology in the interests of biblical truth, or is he rather employing biblical material as a backdrop for his psychological projections?

Chronologically, both in its date or composition and in its subject matter, *Nobodaddy* [1] (1925) merits our first consideration. In this three-act play, Archibald MacLeish (1892-) takes up once more the story of the fall of the first man and woman, a subject which Milton had woven into his *Paradise Lost* more than two centuries before. *Nobodaddy,* though dealing with the same subject treated in mystery plays, differs from these in that it dwells on details which they had left untouched. What MacLeish reads between the lines in the biblical narrative, he embellishes, thus offering points upon which a twentieth-century mind might ruminate.

In the first act, MacLeish elaborates on the temptation. Adam is stirred at the possibilities of fashioning another world out of God's earth. He becomes eloquent as he speaks of his imagined glory:

---

[1] "Nobodaddy" is a term which MacLeish borrowed from William Blake's poem entitled "To Nobodaddy."

> I shall build up a world that will enclose
> His world within it as the curving leaves
> Of lilies hold a rain drop, and I'll set
> Such stars above his stars you will forget
> There was a star in heaven till the bright sheaves
> Of mine were gathered in the field that grows
> East of the evening.[2]

The Act works up to the climax when Eve urges her partner:

> Break off the small fruit there.
> Nearest the branch's end. . . .
> Quick, Adam. (p. 27)

The words that MacLeish puts in the mouth of the man who had eaten of the forbidden fruit are lines fraught with the experiential actuality of sensation:

> Only to touch your hands that make me feel
> My own two hands against them, and your arms
> That are more smooth than mine.
>   And your deep thighs
> That free my body of you, and your breasts
> That set me free—to find you. Oh, to find you—
> Eve, do not go away. (p. 29)

Act II is a dialogue suggestive of fear and poignant recollection of joy that is past. To Adam and Eve, all matter has grown strange, and even God they feel to be a fearful being pervading their darkness. After an act in which the value of the dialogue lies merely in the hinting of the feelings and thoughts of the guilty pair, the play reverts to another act as dramatic as the first. In Act III, the spotlight is on Cain beside whom Abel's figure pales. One of the consequences of the Fall is shown to be the division among Eve's children. The inability to brook a rival that leads to the murder of Abel, the refusal to submit to the Superior Being that makes Cain the unbending rebel searching for God only to strike Him—these are portrayed with a power that lends to the ending of the play a note of exalted tragedy.

---

[2] Archibald MacLeish, *Nobodaddy* (Cambridge: Dunster House, 1926), p. 23.

Although the message of the Bible remains recognizable throughout the play—concupiscence and rebellion as the consequences of the Fall of the first man and woman—what is of interest to the audience is the masterful portrayal of Adam's consuming desire and Cain's overbearing pride. One might say that the merit of the play consists in the convincing interpretation of the psychology of the two main characters rather than in bringing out the biblical message. Adam as presented by MacLeish could be any man strongly conscious of the desirableness of woman, and Cain could be any rebel whose tongue betrays the fire of pride which gnaws at the human heart. Both are portrayed as representatives of the sinning race of man with whom a modern audience can easily identify itself. God's presence is felt especially at the end. He looks on—the "Nobodaddy" who answers curses with imperturbable silence.

From MacLeish's re-creation of Scripture figures in *Nobodaddy* to Giraudoux's interpretation of a biblical heroine in *Judith* (1932), there is a brazen stride toward arbitrariness in the handling of biblical themes. Though MacLeish rivets attention on vivid representation of the characters so that we are hardly aware of the biblical message, his Adam and Cain are nonetheless recognizable as those of the Scriptures, their emotional experiences ring true, and the thoughts they give voice to have a probability that lends them life both in the context of the biblical account as well as in their relation to contemporary reality. When we come to Giraudoux's play, we notice that although he uses more or less the same pattern of events provided by Holy Scripture, his image of the heroine is modelled after the pleasure-loving young girl of today by whom the Judith of the Old Testament is replaced.

Jean Giraudoux (1882–1944) portrays Judith as the modern "fille a la mode." He proceeds to build up her character by what others say of her, and then by what she avows herself to be. The high priest Joachim draws her picture thus:

Le peuple de la rue a choisi Judith, et, plus je songe à elle, plus je croix à Judith. Je la connais, ta nièce. Je l'observe depuis des années.... Elle est belle, et elle le sait.... Et elle sait le prix de la beauté. L'etat-major est peuplé de soupirants qu'elle éconduit. Elle est riche, et elle entend ne pas négliger un seul des avantages ou une seule des joies que donne la fortune. A vingt ans elle a sa cour d'hommes de lettres et sa ferme modèle, son hôpital et ses collections. A la fin de chaque journée, elle a caressé de la main un étalon et un lépreux, des yeux une statue médiocre et un beau statuaire. Des sports et des talents, elle choisit peut-être trop volontiers ceux qui valent des succès et de succès de foule. Elle monte à cheval, et en garçon. Elle danse, et quelquefois dans un lieu public. Elle aime l'entrée brillante au théatre, au restaurant, et main-tenant dans ce harem sans danger qu'on nomme l'hôpital militaire. Je me suis jadis irrité de voir la mode coiffer ce beau cerveau, gonfler cette belle gorge. . . .[3]

There is nothing in this description which would be beyond the com-prehension of the average audience of today. It includes the details by which the fashionable woman is distinguished: beauty and riches that call forth suitors, and the enjoyment of the advantages of her position. She has an intelligence that enables her at twenty to be pop-ular among men of letters, and initiative to embark on worthwhile activities: to have a model farm, even a hospital of her own, and of course, like other women active in society, to have her own collection of art works. Moreover, she engages in spectacular sports; goes riding in men's apparel, dances at times in public, and loves to draw atten-tion to herself by a brilliant entry into the theatre or restaurant, not to speak of the military hospital.

When she actually enters the scene, she fills the room with her liveliness. She has command of brilliant repartee, so that the high priest seems to have a hard time trying to convince her that she is the girl whom the prophets have declared would save them from the terror of Holofernes. Reminded of the prophecy that the most beau-

---

[3] Jean Giraudoux, *Judith* (Paris: Editions Bernard Grasset, 1932), pp. 24-25. The following is my translation:
    The people of the streets have chosen Judith, and the more I think of her, the more I believe in Judith. I know your niece. I have been observing her for years . . . She is beautiful and she knows it . . . And she is aware of the price of beauty. The military staff is filled with suitors whom she attracts. She is rich and she takes care not to neglect the least advantage or the least joy that good fortune can give. At twenty, she has her circle of men of letters and her model farm, her own hospital and her collections. By the end of each day, she has caressed a stallion and a leper with her own hands, with her eyes a mediocre statue as well as fine statues. Among sports and achievements, she has chosen perhaps consciously, those that count for success—the success that means much to the crowds. She rides on horseback and in male attire. She dances, and sometimes in some public place. She loves the brilliant entrance to the theatre or the restaurant, and now in that harmless harem that we call the military hospital. I have already been irritated on seeing her way of dressing her hair, her throat swelling. . . .

tiful and the purest of women would be chosen for the mission, she answers:

> Do they say she would be the most frivolous, the most coquettish, the most changeable? I am all that, too, believe me.[4]

Her true character, however, is unfolded only after she has heard of the desperate plight of the Hebrew soldiers who no longer have an army. From thence on she experiences a number of *volte-faces* which are baffling even to the most alert audience. Almost as if to prove to her lover, Jean, that she can make her own decisions, she resolves: "I shall be the loveliest tonight, that I swear." (p. 57). And she who had at first shown no desire to become the fulfillment of the prophecy soon rises to the situation, giving such abundant play to her imagination that she is surprised at herself. "Already, in advance, by a thousand facets, my eyes see all," she declares. And when asked, "Do you see Holofernes, half asleep, drawing you to his enormous embrace, bending you on him?" she finds herself vividly imagining the situation: "I see him. I touch him. . . . Heavens, where am I?" [5]

And she gets ready to start for the camp of the enemy. Once set on her mission, she no longer fears any dangers. She refuses the substitution offered by the prostitute Suzanne. Her behavior in the mock court set to humiliate her is admirable. Upon realizing the shameful trick that has been played on her, she cries to Holoferness in piercing anguish.

Face to face with this conqueror, she hardly thinks of her nation, and when asked what she desires, she replies, "Nothing. Nothing more." [6] It is Holofernes who reminds her, "You do not wish to speak to me of your god?" "That he manifest himself!" is her answer. "He is sufficiently strong and terrible." The ensuing dialogue shows the process of her gradual separation from the motives that had prompted her to come to the enemy's tent.

---

[4] This translation and those that appear on the following pages are mine. In the original (p. 32):
> Dit-elle la plus frivole, la plus coquette, la plus changeante? Je suis tout cela aussi. Croyez-moi.

[5] *Ibid.*, pp. 67-68:
> Je le vois. Je le touche . . . Je vois une grosse veine bleue qui bat à son cou comme au cou des taureaux. Je le presse du doigt. La face s'empourpre . . . Ciel, où suis-je?

[6] *Ibid.*, p. 152.

"And your brethren? When you left them, a few hours ago, you did not intend to obtain their salvation?"

"Thousands of years have passed since I left them."

"Where do you feel you are?"

"On an islet. In a glade."

"You see. You have guessed it."

"What have I guessed?"

"That there is no god here."

Having described the condition of those who have no god, and the gifts of pleasure which he has to offer her, Holofernes finally asks: "Oh! Judith, what do you desire?" "You know it. . . ." she answers, "to lose myself." Yet, when Holofernes promises to give her what she wants, she cries for pity, for a moment of pause. The wished-for interlude comes in the form of Suzanne who has followed her in a last effort to avert the danger to which she is exposing herself. The interference, however, only serves to harden Judith in her resolution, knowing full well what is about to happen. "God has abandoned me," she says, "I do not know why, but He has abandoned me. . . . He loves the idea of sacrifices among His creatures, He places them in the position, but the details are repugnant to Him. I was too proud in my virtue. He wants it to be squandered without merit."[7]

The psychological changes take place with bewildering rapidity: from indifference regarding a mission to its patriotic acceptance; from fear of being abandoned by God to a night of abandon in an enemy's tent; from unrestrained avowal of guilt to miraculous belief in her own sainthood. The result is a Judith foreign to the Scriptures. To notice the differences between the Old Testament version and Giraudoux's piece is to realize how little of the biblical spirit can remain in a modern play which is yet apparently biblical in its subject matter.

The sequence of events is the same. But the thoughts and feelings animating the two Judiths are as different as scarlet and white. The climax of Giraudoux's piece still involves the slaying of Holofernes. But whereas the biblical Judith had done it in the desire to fulfill a mission from God for her country, Giraudoux's heroine kills a lover in Holofernes for a personal reason: in the despair of ever being able to live a humdrum life again after the night of romance with him. The difference that lies between the two women is that which stands

---

7 *Ibid.,* pp. 153-80.

between the world of the spirit and that of the senses. The first is on the plane of the supernatural, the latter on the level of the sensational.

Giraudoux's method in this play is to take a biblical setting in which a scriptural pattern of events gyrates around a heroine whose speech and manner mark her off as definitely belonging to the present. In the process, the spirit of the Scriptures evaporates, the message is nullified. For the message of the *Book of Judith* is that salvation comes to the Jewish people through the courage and spirit of sacrifice of a woman whose virtue is protected through prayer and prudence. The Judith of the Bible is the woman characterized by dignity, sincerity of purpose as well as womanly grace and wisdom. To all appearances, Giraudoux does not believe in the triumph of a woman's virtue through prayer, if we may judge by his presentation of Judith. His Judith does not really know how to pray. She is a mixture of coquetry and patriotism, of fashion and wit. Belief in her virtue is forced on her by people and events against the evidence of her own better knowledge of herself. To credit Giraudoux's Judith as the authentic biblical heroine would be to discredit the very ideal of sanctity which is at the core of the biblical message. But was this the Judith Giraudoux wished to portray? Or was it to humor his audience that he gave this interpretation of Judith as plausible?

As a historical presentation of the incidents preceding the passage of the Israelites from Egypt, Christopher Fry's play, *The Firstborn,* bears comparison to the two plays just discussed. However, whereas in *Nobodaddy* the playwright made no pretense of weaving a plot, *The Firstborn* is a carefully organized drama with Moses as protagonist. Like Giraudoux, Christopher Fry (1907–   ) takes pains to construct a probable plot, even more closely resembling the biblical narrative; but unlike his French contemporary, the English dramatist presents a Moses who fits in with the picture drawn by the Scriptures. Moreover, while making the soul states of Moses transparent, Fry gives him sufficient individuality to withstand the gaze of today's audiences.

In this attempt to appropriate the story of *Exodus* for its dramatic value, Fry apparently concentrates on the character of Moses. Focusing his attention on this central figure, the dramatist draws the personality of a man with the mission of leading his people from slavery, so that the other personages easily fall into their right positions in relation to him. As leader involved in extremely difficult circumstances, Moses does not become an abstraction. Great as his daring and spiritual strength may be, he is not presented as invulnerable to doubt and hesitation. Described by Ramases as "clear and risen roundly over the hazes,"[8] as one who has the formula of life, Moses answers:

> Clear?
> Evidence of that! Where in this drouthy
> Overwatered world can you find me clarity?
> . . . .
> What language is life? Not one I know.
> A quarrel in God's nature. . . .

As he goes about his mission, he finds the ways of God incomprehensible, and stands in pained puzzlement before the difficulties to be overcome in accomplishing the divine will. Grieved at the death of Ramases which is the result of the Pharaoh's refusal to listen to warnings, Moses exclaims:

> I do not know why the necessity of God
> Should feed on grief; but it seems so. And to know it,
> Is not to grieve less, but to see grief grow big
> With what has died, and in some spirit differently
> Bear it back to life. (p. 88)

Earlier in the play he had said:

> The shadows are too many.

Yet, in the last scene, his closing lines deliver the message of the play which is also the biblical message of hope:

> . . . .
> We must each find our separate meaning
> In the persuasion of our days
> Until we meet in the meaning of the world.
> Until that time. (pp. 89-90)

The attitudes of the three members of Moses' family—his sister Miriam's bitterness and total lack of sympathy to his mission, her son Shendi's refusal to credit Moses' words, Aaron's frequent inability to comprehend that their task is beyond the human—only intensify

---

[8] *The Firstborn* (London: Oxford University Press, 1956), p. 27. Quotations appearing in the following pages are from this edition.

the poignancy of the leader's struggle. The situation perfectly exemplifies the lines from Holy Writ, that a man's enemies are those of his own house. That the Pharaoh should set up obstacles against Moses was hard enough though inevitable; but that members of his own family should not be able to share his burdens must have been still harder. The Moses presented by Fry is a figure of the Redeemer who would save the world from the slavery of sin. Yet, he does not remain a mere figure. An intensely human character, he experiences the conflicting emotions of faith and loyalty to God on the one hand, and a deep and tender attachment to Egypt on the other. Two women in the play suggest this call to his affections: Anath, his foster mother who had brought him up to promising manhood, and Teusret, his lovely foster cousin who is the very picture of the innocent childhood he had known. Moreover, according to Fry himself, "Ramases represented for Moses his own youth as Prince of Egypt and his still remaining love for the Egypt which he is now helping to destroy."[9]

As the personification of Moses' love for Egypt, Ramases deserves the title role. For this drama is typically biblical in its treatment of death attended by hope in the future. The death of Ramases is in reality the tragedy of Moses whose affections are strongly drawn to the Egypt of his youth; and if Moses the leader stands at the threshold of a promised land, it is only at the cost of death to his past and to all the earthly glory it stands for in his affection. Considered by himself, Ramases falls short of the qualities of a tragic character. There is too much gentleness, too much poetry in him, and too little strength to make him stand out as a tragic hero. His death becomes tragic only in relation to Moses and to Seti; considered as the victim of circumstances he does not attempt to avert, this frail prince in the bloom of youth would cut but a pathetic figure.

Seti, the Pharaoh of Egypt, the powerful antagonist of Moses, strangely remains a mere symbolic type. In him Fry embodies the characteristics of the utilitarian dictator who values all things only inasmuch as they serve his purposes. When he breaks the ten years of silence about Moses whom he has considered as belonging to the past, it is because the kingdom is being threatened by an attack of the Libyans. He knows that only Moses can lead his armies to victory, and so he asks Anath to look for her foster son. It is a practical

---

[9] In a letter to the author dated October 29, 1964.

urgency which prompts him to seek reconciliation. Seti can find no words with which to conceal his thoughts. He makes no attempt at dissimulation. His words to Anath, "I need him," have a bluntness which does not lose its quality even when reiterated in "I have found him necessary," and again, "He is essential to my plans." He can think of people only in relation to his designs. Talking about the carefree popularity of Ramases, Seti remarks:

> I'm not altogether at rest in the way he's growing,
> His good graces for no-matter-whom.
> He must learn to let the needs of Egypt rule him. (p. 8)

To this Pharaoh, everything must be subordinated to the glory of Egypt which is identified with himself. He puts this idea of Egypt very directly when he speaks of having brought about the life of his son thus:

> I made life in your mother
> To hand me strength when I should need it. That life
> Was you. (p. 59)

It is the enforced necessity of subservience to his father's goals that oppresses Ramases into the sickening cry:

> I'm to inherit the kingdom
> Of desperate measures, not to be a self
> But a glove disguising your hand. Is there nowhere
> Where I can come upon my own shape
> Between these overbearing ends of Egypt?
> Where am I to look for life? (p. 82)

The complete crystallization of Seti into a symbolic type is prevented only at the last scene when we see him weakening, powerless to avert the heaviest of his misfortunes. In answer to Moses' demand that Ramases be saved by the miracle of their vigorous lives drawn around him, Seti confesses:

> I will do anything
> But all direction is gone. (p. 85)

After a series of maneuvers through which he tried to seek his own objectives, he finds himself baffled, helpless, bereft of all power to aid even his own heir.

Into the three-act play in which the incidents move toward the tragic catastrophe of Ramases' death, Fry has given an interpretation of Moses which, while remaining faithful to the image set down in Holy Scripture, is nonetheless that of an individual whose psychology is understandable to any age. Fry has moreover related the ancient figure of Seti to the modern world by identifying him with totalitarian utilitarianism [10] which has its counterpart in modern politics. Despite the episodic quality of certain scenes, the incidents in the play are sufficiently knit together by their converging toward the catastrophe.

Although Fry's masterful character portrayal of Moses could not fully win over a contemporary audience, *The Firstborn* remains as a noteworthy effort to mold a biblical theme into a work of art. It has the rare distinction of possessing the individualizing stamp of the dramatist's imaginative insight along with great fidelity to the biblical original.

Of the three plays studied so far, it will be noticed that despite the use of a common dramaturgy—the historical presentation made to appeal by means of psychology—the spirit animating them varies enormously. In *Nobodaddy*, the biblical material is a tool for humanism: the focus is on the thoughts and feelings experienced by men at the beginning of time, feelings which are also known to men today. Giraudoux, on the other hand, is not interested in the past; he is evidently intrigued by the character of a modern woman. And to make his creation of this woman live, he uses the biblical background. The result is a world apart from that found in the Bible. It is, in certain parts, a parody of the original. For the dramatist has that in him

> Which could build
> Out of this earth of His another earth. . . .[11]

It is in *The Firstborn* that we find a dramatist doing justice to biblical material in the exercise of his dramatic genius.

In the writing of these three plays, the dramatists took care to give their characters realistic vigor, and to make the logic of the incidents so closely knit as to possess a toughness sufficient to appeal

---

[10] See Derek Stanford, *Christopher Fry—An Appreciation* (London: Peter Nevill, Ltd., 1952), p. 122.
[11] *Nobodaddy*, pp. 17-18.

to an audience influenced by rationalism. Marc Connelly (1890–)
in *The Green Pastures* (1930), and Andre Obey (1892–) in *Noah*
(1931) take a divergent approach. Theirs is the daring strategy of
bypassing the sophistication of Broadway and the Boulevards, and
addressing their audiences directly as "people, poets, and (at least in
make-believe) pure in heart."[12]

As a mystery play, *The Green Pastures* is one of the most old-
fashioned pieces of our century. True to its type, it has "no sense of
period as we think of it: no sense that because this story actually
happened . . . a great many years ago, the people must therefore appear
different."[13] Yet, the ingenuity with which Connelly presents the
Old Testament narrative as "it might be imagined by an old Negro
Preacher"[14] picturing the biblical scenes and characters as the Louisiana
Negro might fancy them, gives the play a charm which is a triumph
of modern psychology.

The play is built on the simple framework of a series of scenes
strung together to bring the Old Testament narrative to the compre-
hension of a Sunday school class. It has no plot, but its episodes are
so developed as to entertain while instructing this very simple audience,
beginning with the scene of Heaven before the creation of man, and
proceeding through the narrative of Adam and Eve, the condition of
the world before the Flood, the passage of the Israelites from Egypt,
and their struggle for the integrity of the Jewish nation. The play
ends with a prophetic note on the Passion.

What the dramatist attempts in *The Green Pastures* is not merely
to re-create characters of the Bible as he imagines them to be, but
more importantly to reconstruct them from the point of view of a
particular narrator addressing himself to a specific group. With its
breathtaking grasp of Negro psychology, and its appeal to Sunday
school associations, the play is capable of disarming the right audience.
It is refreshingly amusing to the Negro spectators who are pleasantly
surprised by the startling similarity of the presentation with their ways

---

12 Francis Fergusson, *The Idea of a Theater* (New York: Doubleday and
Co., 1949), p. 216.
13 E. Martin Browne (ed.), *Religious Drama 2: Mystery and Morality Plays*
(New York: Meridian Books, Inc., 1959), p. 13.
14 Richard A. Cordell (ed.), *Twentieth Century Plays: American* (New
York: The Ronald Press Co., 1947), p. 132.

of life. The non-Negro audience, too, cannot help admiring the naiveté of imagery and the natural turn of expression with which the dramatist portrays Old Testament personages.

Part of the enjoyment of the play comes from the recognition of inconsistencies between the Negro imagination and the reality of the Scriptures. It is delightful to witness the scene of angels at a fish fry which is supposed to signify maximum enjoyment for the Louisiana Negro. The unlimited amount of ten-cent cigars and custards contribute to the idea of abundance which is associated with the notion of heaven. The naive realism of the whole scene is amusing, with the Mammy Angel slapping the back of a girl-cherub who has swallowed a fishbone, with her declaration that so much firmament having been created, the cherubs are getting all wet. Connelly presents the granddaughter of Cain the Sixth as a flirt "reekin' wid cologne." The characters speak and act as their counterparts in the modern world; like Giraudoux in Judith, the dramatist makes no effort whatever to avoid anachronisms, but rather includes them, one might say, on purpose, to the delight of the sympathetic audience.

Richard Cordell has pointed out that "Criticism has not been entirely laudatory" for The Green Pastures. Success in the presentation of biblical scenes from the point of view of a limited ethnic group may be the very cause of prejudice from some quarters. The remark of one Southern woman is an instance: "But who on earth cares about Negro psychology?" In England, too, censors had been persistent in refusing to license the play for public performance, despite the spirited criticism of intelligent British playgoers. Nonetheless, this twentieth-century mystery play has been able to delight people with its local color which is a blending of sunny humor with a "tenderness and quiet dignity"[15] that lifts the piece to a plane of poetic beauty.

If Connelly's appeal is to an audience's love of local color, Andre Obey's is to the histrionic sensibility. To enjoy Noah, the dramatist demands that an audience join him in make-believe. He takes, so to speak, the "coy attitude of the teller of fairy tales."[16] By means of his consistent use of stylization in acting, Obey coaxes his audience to watch scene after scene. Once the onlookers have entered into the spirit of the play, however, they discover that instead

---

15 Ibid., p. 133.
16 Fergusson, op. cit., p. 217.

of the world of the fairy tale they were prepared to watch, it is their own world being represented, with its manifold problems of the family.

In the five scenes that comprise *Noah,* Obey is trying to show us a view of the tragic rhythm of human life. The play opens at the time when the ark is about to be finished, and Noah is getting his last-minute instructions from God whom he hears in snatches. There is the intimacy and realism of daily speech in his address to God, but there is also trust. As the animals approach the ark in pairs, Noah realizes that the time he had been preparing for has come. His family joins him, none too enthusiastic about their new house. The action in the first scene builds up to the dramatic incident of the drought ending by a downpour of rain falling on the man who had laughed in mockery at Noah's prophecy of the deluge.

In the next scene, with the first sunshine on their forty-first day in the ark, the family enjoy themselves on deck, except for Ham whose cynicism is a jarring note. This note of cynicism in the second scene is carried on to the third where Ham's egoism begins to infect the rest: his two brothers, Sem and Japhet, the three girls whom they are to marry, and their mother who takes their side. The words that Noah speaks to the animals at the end of the scene are really being spoken to himself:

> Call to Him, yes. Let's raise our voices. I'm willing. But not in fear. Not in anger. Make it a song to please His ear. Lord!—Lord!—Lord!!...
>
> Once more, Mates! But without a shadow of fear or doubt. Now! All together. One voice! One soul! Lord!—Lord!—Lord!—...
>
> That's good. Have faith now. Quiet. Quiet down, everybody.... There, there, rest. I'm tired, children.... Here on the boundless, bottomless, motionless waters we'll build a towering monument of patience—That'll attract His attention. Just as an oak attracts lightning. There, now—There—
>
> He must see how much we know—of everything in the world—that—slow—...The birds are singing—They haven't sung for a long time—God is not far away, children—(Act II, Sc. 2)

The storm in the first scene of Act III precipitates the feeling of rebellion which has been rising in the family against Noah. Nobody believes in him now—not even his own wife. His faith tells him that land is surely near, and he releases the dove—"the little white soul on wings." After moments of disbelief on the part of the youngsters, the dove comes back bearing a fresh green twig with three little leaves. Mama Noah, overcome with repentance for her disbelief, falls on her knees before her husband. But the rest are lost in their excited anticipation of release from their long confinement in the ark.

The last scene contains the leitmotif of the return to the earth: "All lives go down the mountain"—by pairs the young people, after a quarrel among themselves, a wild dance followed by hasty embraces, follow diverging paths. And Noah is left alone with a wife who has completed the cycle of life with her return to childish ways.

The play ends as it has begun, with Noah addressing himself once more to God in his puzzlement:

> Yes—Ah! How shall I start?... It has been hard—... It's true; it has been hard!—Ah! Well, You must admit that my faith in You is supremely patient—Do you hear me? Yes, I say that You have given me hard knocks. Maybe You've gone beyond what I call sportsmanship. You've taken me from my garden and cast me on a rock, alone with a dozen ways of dying. But I'm not complaining—Hahaha!—That'll be all right—You'll see. I'll find a way out. Yes, God, I'll get out. I warn You; I've given up trying to understand. But that doesn't matter. Not a bit. Go on, I'm following You! March on! March on! Only I ask You to come to me once in a while. Will You? Let me hear Your voice now and then or just let me feel Your breath or simply let me have Your light. Oh, Lord, shed Your light upon my daily job! Let me have the impression—the *feeling*—*Your assurance*—that You are satisfied, will You? We must be satisfied. Isn't that so? I am satisfied. (He shouts) I am satisfied. (He attacks the ark with his hatchet) I am satisfied! (He sings) When the boat goes well, all goes well. Are You satisfied? (The seven colors of the RAINBOW appear in the background) That's fine.

Beneath the surface naiveté of Obey's make-believe, there runs the powerful movement of the analogue which gives the play profundity of meaning. What makes the play capture an audience is its realistic representation, through the cultivated art of the actor, of "the rich and bitter emotional relationship of the family." We see in it the perpetual conflicts between age and youth, the energetic pride of the young, the patient wisdom of age, the complementary character of male and female in bearing the burdens of life, the ever-recurring emotional rhythms of enthusiasms and depressions, of sadness and joy, the pairing off of uncertainty and hope. But above all, there is the assumption that the relationship between the individual and God is real.[17] By an imaginative reconstruction of each character and episode in the biblical narrative, the author has succeeded in giving them their "sensuous and emotional immediacy." In so doing, Obey has given us a biblical play which finds its place in our age as an analogue of the family. It is an example of a subtle art form that hides a severe meaning beneath a cloak of childlike simplicity.

EXPRESSION OF MODERN IDEOLOGIES

Utterly different in dramaturgy are the two plays to be considered next. Bernard Shaw (1856–1950) in *Back to Methuselah* (1921) and Eugene O'Neill (1888–1953) in *Lazarus Laughed* (1926) do not make use of the historical method of presenting biblical themes; neither do they make it their principal aim to subject biblical personages to psychological analysis. What they do is to take the biblical material and use it as a point of departure for the presentation of ideas.

Considered by Shaw to be his crowning work, *Back to Methuselah* makes a pretentious volume of three hundred pages of which more than sixty are devoted to the preface. The central idea of the play is the application of what Shaw called "Creative Evolution," an idea which he derived from the French biologist Jean Baptiste de Monet de Lamarck (1744–1829) and Samuel Butler (1835–1902), the English novelist, essayist and critic who wrote on numerous subjects including evolution. In *Man and Superman* (1903), Shaw had argued that the Life Force worked through sexual selection so that human beings and human life might be indefinitely improved through breeding a superior type of individual—the Superman. Twenty years later, by the time he wrote *Back to Methuselah,* he had lost faith in this theory and decided that to reach intellectual maturity through the innate tendencies of development and transformation claimed by Lamarck, men need a span of life consisting of 300 years and more. The extension of life would enable men to "re-create human society and give a new meaning and dignity to the life of the race."[18] Moreover, such an extension would be possible once an individual is convinced that longer existence is essential for the upliftment of the human race. The prophecy which

---

17 *Ibid.,* p. 220.
18 Homer E. Woodbridge, *G. B. Shaw: Creative Artist* (Carbondale: Southern Illinois University Press, 1965), p. 107.

Shaw seems to take very seriously is that men by force of will and mind can find a way of prolonging life and becoming vortices of thought.

The play consists of five parts, each of which is a play in itself. Thus, Woodbridge calls the piece a miracle cycle, being a dramatization of important events in the past, present and future of the human race as imagined by Shaw. The term *miracle* applied to the piece is farfetched. Yet, Shaw seems to have entertained a notion that the five parts of *Back to Methuselah* comprise the prophetic books to the modern bible, and that in writing this play, he was drawing, as he had not been able to do heretofore, "an iconography of the religion"[19] of this time.

The first part, consisting of two acts, is Shaw's version of the biblical theme of the garden of Eden. In the opening scene, Adam and Eve are confronted for the first time with the fact of death in the death of a fawn. Seeing it, Eve experiences the fear that should this happen to them, only plants and animals would exist in Paradise. Something in her tells her that they must not cease to exist. Adam, on the other hand, is afraid that if death came to Eve, he would be left alone—alone with himself. To him, the greatest horror is to be alone with himself forever. It is the serpent who teaches Eve the secret of renewing herself over and over again by birth. As Eve listens, the expression of curiosity on her face changes into one of shame.

There is a long lapse of time; the second act in Part I presents Eve's problem in her sons. Cain has murdered his brother Abel; moreover, he is obsessed by the desire to kill, kill, kill. And only his esteem for his mother prevents him from striking his father. Yet Eve continues to dream of other possibilities among her descendants. The Life Force in her makes her keep on hoping for the time when man may no longer live on bread alone but on something else: on manna— the "food drawn down from heaven, made out of the air, not dug dirtily from the earth." But she realizes that men, to be able to eat manna, must live long enough.

The program of extending human life to centuries is expounded in Part II: "Gospel of the Brothers Barnabas." In the presence of the politicians, Lubin and Burge, Haslam the Rector, and his girl friend Savvy, Conrad and Franklyn Barnabas explain their program

---

[19] In the preface to the play.

for humanity. Lubin is impressed by the possibility of using the program for an election campaign. The rest have not been particularly touched by the argument, except Savvy whose belief is nonetheless tinged by doubts. As the exposition of the doctrine of Creative Evolution, Part II is nondramatic and would have no justification in forming part of a play. However, it is essential to the whole inasmuch as the theory it proposes is shown in its first fulfillment in the succeeding parts.

After sixty pages of flat dialogue in Part II, the dramatic moments in the next scene come as a relief. We discover in Part III: "The Thing Happens" that the Archbishop of York is none other than the rector, Haslam, who is actually in his third century of life and has been assuming various important positions in the country ever since we became acquainted with him as a visitor to the Barnabas Brothers. Moreover, we find out that Mrs. Lutestring, the Domestic Minister, is none other than the parlor maid in Part II. Probably to bring out the notion that England is in need of being saved by people who can live longer than the ordinary span of life, Shaw conceives of England as being ruled by foreigners, among whom are a Chinese who is the Chief Secretary of State, and a Negress who is the Minister of Health, with whom the President is in love.

Parts IV and V develop possibilities for the time when the extension of life has become the common practice of men. In Part IV, "The Tragedy of an Elderly Gentleman" (3000 A.D.), the British Isles have become the home of the "long-livers" whereas the Commonwealth has transferred its capital to Baghdad. The fame of the oracle in Britain attracts many visitors among the "short-livers" who have a rough time in the hands of the "long-livers." The last part carries one to a time "As Far as Thought Can Reach" (31,920 A.D.). The world has become a place for Ancients who, like Methuselah, live hundreds of years. People have invented a way of painless generation making the human egg fall from the mother until the child is ready to be born; and when the infant comes out of its eggshell, it has the appearance of a youth of seventeen. Thenceforth, it devotes four years to the pleasures of youth, to art and science, after which it becomes an Ancient who is engrossed only in thought. The ghosts of Adam and Eve, Cain and the Serpent, and Lilith conclude the play with their comments. Eve is dissatisfied with mankind for shirking all suffering, even that of generation which she had borne patiently. Adam criticizes men for wishing to get rid of their bodies in order to become only whirlpools of pure intelligence. Cain laments the disappearance of the warriors while philosophers whom he calls the weaker men inhabit the earth. The Serpent is satisfied because "now there is no evil; and wisdom and good are one." Lilith, who is Shaw's substitute for God, summarizes the progress of mankind, knows that men will become the whirlpool which is all life and no matter, and declares:

> I will have patience with them still; though I know well that when they attain it they shall become one with me and supersede me, and Lilith will be only a legend and a lay that has lost its meaning. Of life only is there no end; and though of its million starry mansions many are empty and many still unbuilt, and though its vast domain is as yet unbearably desert, my seed shall one day fill it and master its matter to its uttermost confines. And for what may be beyond, the eyesight of Lilith is too short. It is enough that there is a beyond.

It is evident that Shaw's version has taken all the meaning out of the biblical narrative, offering in its place "not much more than a picture of Eve as the agent of the Life Force."[20] He presents an Eden without the temptation, without the disobedience, without the Fall, and still more, without God, unless we think of the Voice that Adam heard as signifying God. Although the dramatist places Adam and Eve in Eden at the opening of his play, the condition in which we find them is not the bliss of innocence; and although he makes no mention of their fall, he shows Adam as already tired of himself, a state which is generally considered a consequence of original sin. Possessing nothing of the spirit of the Bible, Shaw's opening scenes, it must be admitted, have an intensity not unworthy of the state of the first man and woman. Yet, the biblical material is used not for its own sake, but as a starting point in the dramatist's demonstration of the theory of Creative Evolution. He wanted to show the development of the human race in the expression of the Life Force, and thought of the Garden of Eden as the most plausible beginning. An experienced dramatist that he was, Shaw could not have had any illusions that the play would succeed on the stage. But he wanted to reach a wider audience of readers, so he adopted the dramatic form. At the end of the play, the ghosts of Adam and Eve stalk the stage once more.

---

[20] Woodbridge, *op. cit.*, p. 109.

We may say that in Shaw's *Back to Methuselah* the biblical material is a mere ghost of the Scriptures. The life of the Book does not pulse through it.

If Shaw espoused the Lamarckian ideology of Creative Evolution for his play, O'Neil drew his ideas for *Lazarus Laughed* from Nietzsche's theory of Eternal Recurrence. Indeed, we may say that this play with its complicated design of choruses and masks is a demonstration of the ideas stated by the German philosopher in his first book, *Die Geburt der Tragodie* (1872). The point of attack in this play is at the time when Lazarus has risen from the dead, and his family and friends are getting ready to hold a feast in his honor. Back to life, Lazarus has not yet quite lost the vision of the life beyond the grave. Then, the crowd imitates his wife Miriam's repetition of the words Christ had used in calling him to life, "Lazarus, come forth!", to which there issues the answer, "Yes!" But when his father proposes a toast "To my son, Lazarus, whom a blessed miracle has brought back from death," he declares, "No! There is no death!"— a declaration which surprises the crowd all the more because he says it as he laughs softly, "with a strange unearthly calm in a voice that is like a loving whisper of hope and confidence." And when pressed to tell them "What is beyond there?" he replies in a voice of loving exaltation:

> There is only life! I heard the heart of Jesus laughing in my heart; "There is Eternal Life in No," it said, "and there is the same Eternal Life in Yes! Death is the fear between!" And my heart reborn to love of life cried "Yes!" and I laughed in the laughter of God!

And the dramatist writes:

> (He begins to laugh, softly at first—a laugh so full of a complete acceptance of life, a profound assertion of joy in living, so devoid of all self-consciousness or fear, that it is like a great bird song triumphant in depths of sky, proud and powerful, infectious with love, casting on the listener an enthralling spell. The crowds in the room are caught by it. Glancing sideways at one another, smiling foolishly and self-consciously, at first they hesitate, plainly holding themselves in for fear of what the next one will think.)

But when Lazarus invites them saying, "Laugh! Laugh with me! Death is dead! Fear is no more! There is only life! There is only laughter!" the chorus re-echoes his words which the crowd gradually joins in a "great, full-throated paean as the laughter of Lazarus rises higher and higher."

In the second scene, some months later, the house of Lazarus, which has become known as the House of Laughter, is thronged with his followers. Their laughter, accompanied by dancing and singing, has begun to baffle the onlookers who are divided into the Nazarenes (followers of Christ) and the Orthodox Jews. The aged blame Lazarus for bringing the youth from their work in the fields; the Nazarenes accuse him of disloyalty to Christ whose death does not impress him at all. The excitement leads to a riot in which the Nazarenes and the Orthodox fall on one another calling the attention of the Romans who send soldiers to quell the disturbance. In the skirmish which takes place, the members of Lazarus' family die, and yet he insists that there is no death. And when the Roman Centurion declares that he has orders to bring him to Caesar, an exultant "Yes!" is the answer accompanied by a laughter issuing from the depths of his exalted spirit—a laughter which is once more echoed by the chorus and by his followers, and even by the soldiers. But as soon as he has left the scene, the spell is lost, and his followers forget his laughter. In a dull, resigned terror they cry:

> Death slinks out
> Of his grave in the heart!
> Ghosts of fear
> Creep back in the brain!
> We remember fear.
> We remember death!

The Second Act consists of two scenes in which Lazarus is acclaimed, first as a god—Dionysus—in Athens, and then as a Caesar in Rome where the Legion desires to make him their god. But Lazarus' question: "What is Caesar?" makes them at a loss what to answer. Then Lazarus says, "When men make gods, there is no God." From scene to scene Lazarus grows younger while Miriam, his wife, becomes older. She cannot understand why his laughter can continue when his followers whom he has loved have died:

> They were like your children—and they have died. Must you not mourn
> for them?...They are gone from us. And their mothers weep.

And Lazarus answers: "But God, their Father, laughs!"

In the Third Act, Lazarus is brought before Tiberius Caesar. To find out whether Lazarus can raise the dead to life, Tiberius makes Miriam eat a poisoned peach. Moreover, the onlookers feel certain that should the woman he loved die, Lazarus would surely cease laughing. Despite a dramatic moment when the wife seems to come back temporarily to life, they find that Lazarus has no power over death. Yet, when, after an expression of apparent pain he kisses Miriam, his face becoming radiant with new faith and joy, and they hear him laughing again, there is panic in the court, each one laughing his own kind of laughter as he listens to Lazarus' words: "But there is no death, no fear, no loneliness! There is only God's Eternal Laughter! His Laughter flows into the lonely heart!"

In spite of themselves, several individuals conceive an admiration for Lazarus. Caligula, Tiberius Caesar's heir, frequently asserts that he is in love with Lazarus. Tiberius himself is led to confess the crimes that filled his past, and to long for the innocence that was his before he learned to detest his mother. Pompeia, his mistress, makes love to Lazarus but is disappointed that he does not love her as an individual but as Woman in general.

Momentary stirrings of admiration give way to fear toward this superhuman laugher. Tiberius wants to see whether Lazarus would be able to laugh even in the throes of death. Burnt alive over a huge pile of faggots, Lazarus is gagged so that he would not be able to laugh. But curiosity makes Tiberius command that the gag be removed so that Lazarus might answer the question: "What is beyond there?" The reply is given with surpassing clearness and exaltation: "Life! Eternity! Stars and dust! God's Eternal Laughter!" The response to this statement is varied. Tiberius declares that he no longer fears death; he counsels the people not to fear Caesars but to laugh them away. Caligula feels that he has been betrayed as the future Caesar; he stabs Lazarus but is immediately filled with a madman's conflicting emotions: remorse, terror, ferocity, admiration.

It is clear that O'Neill was interested in the biblical theme of the dead man brought back to life, as a demonstration of the theory of eternal rebirth. Death is a kind of Dionysiac dismemberment which marks the end of individuation, "the shattering of the individual and

his fusion with the original Oneness."[21] The Lazarus of O'Neill is not
the follower of Christ, not a believer in Him as the Son of God, but
one who believes in "the laughing god" within man. To Lazarus as
O'Neill presents him, "Man remains! Man slowly arises from the past
of the race of men that was his tomb of death! For Man death is not!
Man, Son of God's Laughter, is!" (Act IV, Sc. 1) As the god Dionysus,
reborn, Lazarus rises from death to convince people that "despite
every phenomenal change, life is at bottom indestructibly joyful and
powerful,...."[22] On the surface, there is in the play something of the
biblical attitude of the acceptance of life. But the spirit in which the
acceptance is made is different. O'Neill's Lazarus accepts life with its
alterations because it is a means of laughing with God. Death is denied
and so is suffering. To the man of the Bible, however, death is a fact
and so is suffering, and these, too, are accepted along with life because
they are a means of making us godlike and enabling us to enter into
eternal life.

Besides embodying the idea of Eternal Recurrence, O'Neill also
exemplifies the signs of Dionysiac rapture, both in Lazarus and in
the crowds and various groups that watch him in the different scenes.
Describing Man while he experiences the transport of the Dionysiac
state, Nietzsche says:

> Each of his gestures betokens enchantment; through his sounds of a
> supernatural power, the same power which makes the animals speak and
> the earth render milk and honey. He feels himself to be godlike and
> strides with the same elation and ecstasy as the gods he has seen in his
> dreams....[23]

This is just how O'Neill presents Lazarus—a man who impresses even
the most hardened men with a power that transcends the natural:
"How does that Jew make that light come from him, I wonder?"
exclaims a Roman senator in Act II. Later, Crassus cannot quite
explain the impression given him by Lazarus: "I do not understand.
But there is god in it somewhere—a god of peace—a god of happiness!..." There is in his laughter an exultation that is felt and loved.

---

21 Friedrich Nietzsche, "The Birth of Tragedy from the Spirit of Music,"
translated by Francis Golffing, included in B.H. Clark's *European Theories
of the Drama* (New York: Crown Publishers, Inc., c. 1965), p. 300.
22 *Ibid.*, p. 298.
23 *Ibid.*

Tiberius Caesar, despite his wish that there should be no laughter in his presence, is forced to admit, "Yet I like thy laughter. It is young. Once I laughed somewhat like that—so I pardon thee. I will laugh at thee in return." In the last scene, Pompeia is hypnotized by his laughter and descends the steps like a sleep-walker saying: "I hear his laughter calling. I must go to him."

As to the choruses and crowds which are presented in the play, they are indeed what Nietzsche calls "an entire multitude agitated by Dionysos." The laughter of Lazarus casts an enchantment that spreads like fire; and in the rapture which the followers experience, there is a Lethean element in which the individual forgets his past and becomes merged into a "chorus of the transformed who have become timeless servants of their god and live outside all social spheres." This oblivion of everyday reality makes the Aged Jew complain in Act I:

> They have no respect for life! When I said in kindness, "You must go back to work," they laughed at me! Ha—! "We desire joy. We go to Lazarus," they said—and left my fields! I begged them to stay—with tears in my eyes! I even offered them more money! They laughed! "What is money? Can the heart eat gold?" They laughed at money! Ha-ha—!

This state of transport, however, is but temporary, experienced only during the presence of Lazarus. As soon as he leaves them, the same Lethean element that made them oblivious of daily life also makes them forget the laughter that had been the expression of exaltation. And their fears return.

It has been pointed out that during the thirty odd years since its publication, the play has had only one production, and that this is understandable, as "the hero spends a large proportion of the play just laughing—sometimes alone, in harmony with a chorus of over a hundred people." Nonetheless, one of the most enthusiastic comments came from Oscar Cargill who wrote that *Lazarus Laughed* is "the supreme piece of drama of modern times," a pronouncement said to have been made mainly on the grounds that "it uses so fully the ideas which Jung set out in his Psychological Types."[24]

As a theatrical production, it must be granted that *Lazarus Laughed* should be impressive, although it is too demanding. The movement on the stage is rhythmic, and the spectacle, colorful. The

---

[24] Gascoigne, *op. cit.,* p. 109.

masks that change from Jewish to Greek and then to Roman types, all the while retaining the expression of the seven general types of character, are a distinguishing feature of the production. The cries of the crowd have the quality of ritual: the voices—reminiscent of the dithyramb—become a chorus of the transformed at the approach of a god. As a work of art that champions ideas, the play is more subtle than Shaw's *Back to Methuselah,* gaining in beauty by the poet's consistent vision of a god and his followers united in joyous laughter, and by the melody that runs in Lazarus' words as well as in the songs of the choruses.

As we study the two plays that aim at demonstrating modern ideas, we notice that although they start with very different biblical material, Shaw and O'Neill are both concerned with supermen. In making a dramatic application of the theory of creative evolution, Shaw has drawn a picture of highly developed supermen, the Methuselahs of the future, whose lives are to be prolonged to centuries by the utmost use of the Life Force which was already felt by Eve at the beginning of time. Shaw's ancients are withered, breastless beings who strive to make their activity pure thinking freed from matter. In their cold and intellectual detachment we may find something to admire, but nothing to love. O'Neill's superman is Dionysus reborn. As such, Lazarus is given the dignity of the dreamer, the detachment of wisdom, together with the compassionate tenderness of one who loves all men. He is, therefore, a much more lovable figure than the ancients of Shaw's drama. But neither in the Methuselahs of Shaw's "prophetic books" nor in the Lazarus of O'Neill's piece for the "theatre of tomorrow" can we recognize the heroes of the Bible whose names they bear. Unlike the biblical heroes whose final participation in the divine life is the result of their faith in and cooperation with Christ's work of Redemption, the men of Shaw's Creative Evolution march on in progress till the day they will be able to replace God; the Man whom O'Neill presents as having risen from death preaches that men should bring out the god in the self so as to be able to join in the laughter of God.

One might think that these dramatists, engrossed as they were in the thought of men as gods, naturally went back to the Bible to find points of departure. According to Shaw, with the Life Force that was already in Eve, men, by sheer force of intelligence and will, work out their way to divinity. To O'Neill, the divine is already in man—like Lazarus, he has but to bring it out in a perpetually recurrent life. In presenting his ideas in dramatic form, Shaw is often expository in method, whereas O'Neill is lyrical.

INTEGRATION OF BIBLICAL THEMES INTO HISTORICAL ACTION AND CONTEMPORARY SITUATION

Among the well-known theories of T.S. Eliot (1888–1965) we come across what he calls the "mythical method." It was in connection with James Joyce's novel that the critic considered myth as "a way of controlling, of ordering, of giving a shape and a significance to the immense panorama of futility and anarchy which is contemporary history."[25] He further declared that Joyce was adopting "a method which others must pursue after him." Among those "others," Eliot stands out most prominently, for almost all his plays make use of Greek myth.

The Orestes myth with the theme of pursuit by the Furies can be recognized in his earliest play, *Sweeney Agonistes* (1932) as well as in *The Family Reunion* written some seven years later. Eliot himself announced the Greek source of *The Cocktail Party* to the *Alcestis* of Euripides in which Heracles at the commencement of the play has his counterpart in Sir Harcourt-Reilly who arrives as the Unidentified Guest. Like Heracles, he actually aids in the solution of the couple's problem. *The Confidential Clerk* goes back to Euripides' *Ion* for its source, *Ion* being the story of a misplaced child, as Colby is, in Eliot's drama. Stressing the idea of expiation by prolonged suffering and devotion to the designs of Providence, *The Elder Statesman* is reminiscent of *Oedipus at Colonus*. Thus, in these plays, Eliot takes a situation as a frame of events from Greek myth, and transposes these to a contemporary setting to create a totally modern play with characters who fall within the sphere of our experience.

In *Murder in the Cathedral,* however, although the fixed form of Greek tragedy is discernible in the plot, Eliot has made the sequence of events "to conform to the Christian interpretation of that pattern in the biblical lore surrounding Christ's Crucifixion and Resurrection."[26] What is evident to the audience is a biblical theme transposed

---

25 In "Ulysses, Order, and Myth," *Dial* lxxv (November 1923), pp. 480-83.
26 Carol H. Smith, *T.S. Eliot's Dramatic Theory and Practice* (Princeton: Princeton University Press, 1963), p. 104.

to a historical situation. Out of the mass of events surrounding Thomas a Becket's martyrdom, Eliot fashions a pattern which definitely belongs to the Bible.

Nowhere else has Eliot succeeded so well in establishing and integrating various levels of significance in accordance with his ideas of poetry for the theatre,[27] as in this stylized dramatization of a historical event. On the surface, *Murder in the Cathedral* is a representation of the martyrdom of Henry II's chancellor. It is a plot which can be grasped by the simplest audience. For the more sophisticated, Eliot offers a psychological presentation of the character of Becket, with his conflicts, spiritual and otherwise, before his death. Then there is the level of phrasing and of rhythm for the more literary and the more musically sensitive. But for the auditors of still greater sensitivity and understanding, there is the plane of meaning which reveals itself gradually, for underneath the structure of events, there is the deeper meaning developed by an analogy between the martyr and Christ. The temptation of Thomas is evidently symbolic of the temptation of Christ. When the Fourth Tempter enters, the words with which Thomas greets him show that he himself was aware of the similarity between his temptations and his Master's:

> Who are you? I expected
> Three visitors, not four.

Inasmuch as Christ had had only three temptations as recorded in Holy Scripture, the coming of a fourth tempter had not been expected. Moreover, the Gospel according to St. Matthew gives us the Sermon on the Mount soon after the narrative of the temptation. So does Becket's Christmas sermon follow his temptation, showing how his triumph in the spiritual struggle had prepared him to face martyrdom, as his sermon implies.

The most obvious analogy in the play is discernible between the Crucifixion of Christ and the murder of Thomas. Both were put to death on account of the jealousy of men desirous of power in this world. The words of the Canterbury martyr recall those of Christ who had called Himself the Good Shepherd laying down His life for His

---

27 Cf. Eliot, *The Use of Poetry and the Use of Criticism* (London: Faber and Faber Ltd., 1933), pp. 146-47.

flock. Urged by the priests to go into the cathedral and close the door on his enemies, the Archbishop answers:

> They shall find the shepherd there; the
> flock shall be spared. (p. 70)

To the reader acquainted with the Gospels, these lines are at once identified with those spoken by Christ when Judas and the band of soldiers accosted Him in the Garden of Gethsemane. He had asked them then that His disciples be spared. In the same vein, Thomas says to the knights who are about to lay hands on Him:

> For my Lord I am now ready to die,
> That his Church may have peace and liberty.
> Do with me as you will, to your hurt and shame;
> But none of my people, in God's name,
> Whether layman or clerk, shall you touch.
> This I forbid. (p. 75)

The last words of Thomas:

> Now to Almighty God, to the Blessed Mary ever Virgin, to the Blessed John the Baptist, the holy apostles Peter and Paul, to the blessed martyr Denys and to all the Saints, I commend my cause and that of the Church. (p. 76)

are a paraphrase of Christ's final cry on the Cross:
    "Father, into Thy Hands I commend my spirit" (Lk. xxii, 46) interwoven with the words of the "Confiteor" familiar to the ordinary Christian.

After the lament of the chorus and the prose speeches which the knights deliver in defense of their deed of violence, the chanting of the priests proceeds from darkness to light, from natural sorrow over their leader's death to thanksgiving to God for having given them one more Saint in Canterbury.

The paean of praise with which the play ends suggests Thomas' entrance into the ranks of sainthood which parallels the resurrection of Christ, and is the Christian version of the apotheosis in Greek ritual drama.

If Eliot's original intention was "to portray the impact of the spiritual principle on the lives of men in a form which would be artistically ordered without losing contact with actual experience,"[28] it would seem as if he departed from this basic dramatic goal in *Murder in the Cathedral.* Yet, according to Eliot himself, the play was written as anti-Nazi propaganda, pointing up the "desire to save the Christian world from attacks of rival secular ideologies."[29]

Eliot's contribution to modern drama through the play, to quote Carol Smith, consists in the creation of an ordered whole, "a rhythmic and proportioned totality forming a complete emotional and ideological whole."[30] It is doubtful whether he could have accomplished this without his use of the undergirding biblical analogy.

Whereas Eliot made use of the biblical theme in order to give meaning to events belonging to the past, other writers transpose a biblical situation to the present, thereby creating a truly modern play whose physical dimensions are of the present, but whose symbolical dimensions extend from the past through modern times.

To illustrate this point, we take Giraudoux once more because the consideration of one of his plays with a biblical theme transposed to a modern situation gives us a chance to observe how this method differs from that which we have seen him employ in *Judith,* namely, the transposition of a modern character to a biblical background, producing the integration of two disparate entities through psychological presentation.

In Giraudoux's one-act play, *Cantique de Cantiques* (1938), the setting is, as the playwright whimsically puts it, at one of the luxurious cafés in France, "overlooking woodlands, or perhaps the Seine"— the place does not matter. What Giraudoux wants to evoke is atmosphere that should be conducive to the serenity which Monsieur le President is looking forward to as he waits for "the most charming of young women."

It is a conversational piece in which hardly any action takes place outside of human decisions. In the witty texture of the conversation and in the ingenious dexterity of Giraudoux in suggesting the rich complexity of a woman's character, the play has its appeal.

To the modern woman, Giraudoux gives the name of Florence. With her elderly lover, Monsieur le President, she has made an

---

28 Smith, *op. cit.,* p. 31.
29 *Ibid.*
30 *Ibid.,* p. 50.

appointment for a rendezvous at this spot of serenity. What the president desired was a moment beyond the earthly, an experience which would serve as an intermission between the duties of his career and the drab routine of the home. The shock that jars him from this complacent dream comes through the information that Florence gives him regarding her forthcoming marriage with the young man Jerome who introduces himself to the president.

So far, there seems to be no trace of biblical material in the play. When Florence arrives and is left with her elderly lover, her complaints regarding Jerome, the younger one, are so endless as to stir some feelings of hope still unquenched in the president's breast. Yet, the entrance of gypsies interrupting Florence's lament is sufficient to change her mood. The gypsies gone, she can no longer talk in the same strain. She now speaks of Jerome's good qualities, and feels impelled to give back Monsieur le President all the jewels he had offered her on various occasions.

The feelings of both softly blend into one once again as they dwell on those anniversaries. Monsieur asks her to take those jewels back, if only as a secret kept even in her marriage with Jerome. And gradually, Florence's feelings for the President change, until she asks him to take her for it is he whom she loves. It is at this point that we notice the playwright deliberately stirring biblical echoes. The cashier and the waiter by turns remind Florence that Jerome is coming back to fetch her. Wholly unpoetical as the speech of the café employees has been up to the present, their recitation of lines reminiscent of the "Song of Songs" serves to make us aware that these are but a scintillation of the undercurrent of Florence's feelings even at the very time she is asking the President to take her with him. Victor, the waiter, says, "The young man is on his way, Mr. President." And the cashier adds:

> He is crossing the lawns. Tiger and Bismarck,
> our terrible wolf-hounds, leap around his feet.
> How gentle is his look; he has killed a bee.
> How lightly he runs; he is trampling the flowers.[31]

---

[31] Quoted from the translation of John Raikes in the *Tulane Drama Review,* III (May 1959) 4, p. 103.

The rhythm and imagery of the biblical original are readily noticeable. The parallel is evident if we but recall some lines from the scriptural text:

> I hear my Beloved.
> See how he comes
> leaping on the mountains,
> bounding over the hills.
> My Beloved is like a gazelle,
> like a young stag.
> . . . .
> Come then, my love,
> my lovely one, come.
> . . . .
> Catch the foxes for us,
> the little foxes
> that make havoc of the vineyards,
> for our vineyards are in flower.
>
> My beloved is mine and I am his.
> He pastures his flock among the lilies.[32]

Florence's next words about their ridding themselves of their weapons, "Enlevons notre armure," is an indication that she is succumbing to the attractions of her young lover again.

The comments of the Specture of Jewels would seem to symbolize the faint appeal which the wealth of the elderly lover still has for Florence. But he loses the strength of his influence as Jerome approaches. And when Jerome asks Florence, "Are you ready?" her answer is of course that she is. He asks her to say goodbye to Monsieur le President, which she does. And she leaves, one might think, with some traces of connivance with the President, until all of a sudden she comes back with apologies for having taken his purse with her unawares. All his jewels are once more returned to him, and their ties are now entirely severed. As in the "Song of Songs," the young lady leaves her royal lover to follow the young man whom she loves despite his poverty.

In this one-act play, Giraudoux is making use of biblical material as a point of reference outside the petty situation of a French café.

---

32 From *The Canticle of Canticles* also known as *The Song of Songs*. The version used is that of *The Jerusalem Bible* (London: Darton, Longman & Todd, 1966), pp. 994-95.

The analogy between an interlude of life and a biblical situation provides an enriching dimension to an incident in contemporary life that would otherwise be merely banal. As in *Judith,* however, Giraudoux is here not so much interested in the biblical theme in itself, as in employing it as a means of bringing out his image of the modern woman's intriguing incomprehensibility of psychology. The message of the playwright is spoken by none other than Florence:

> The gayest woman in the world has to proclaim her despair at some time in her life. It's a physical reaction, nothing to do with the soul.[33]

To Giraudoux, there is nothing mysterious in the behavior of woman. The "Song of Songs" in its modern context is, according to the author, merely the outpouring of the sentiments which a woman experiences at certain moments in her life, out of physical necessity. *Cantique de Cantiques* is indeed the "canticle" of Florence, with its cadence swelling in murmurs of complaint, then ebbing into an awareness of her happiness, rising with nostalgic memories of pleasure with an elderly lover, and subsiding once again into the reality of fondness for her younger lover who is really the stronger of her two loves.

Fry goes further in his attempt to integrate biblical themes into contemporary action. If Giraudoux in *Cantique de Cantiques* confined himself to the simple motif of the woman's choice of a younger lover in preference to a wealthy king, Fry devises a highly complicated structure through the interweaving into the contemporary situation, representative biblical themes covering the period between the Fall, and the coming of Christ. It is a highly ambitious design that almost baffles analysis.

In his previous pieces, Fry had shown a tendency to consider the contemporary world as essentially unpoetic. His angle of preference when writing comedies, tragedies as well as religious pieces had been in the direction of materials provided by the past. His first drama on a biblical theme, *The Firstborn,* is written in the context of the past although interpretation may show its relevance to the present. Now, his technique in *A Sleep of Prisoners* marks a departure from his usual mode of dramaturgy. This time, he deals with contemporary

---

[33] John Raikes' translation. See note 31. The original is as follows:
La femme la plus gaie un beau jour clame son désespoir; la femme la plus heureuse, sa détresse. C'est une function de son corps, pas de son âme. (p. 73 of the Bernard Grasset edition, c. 1939)

action which involves four British enlisted men (Corporal Joe Adams, Privates Tim Meadows, David King and Peter Able) who have been captured and are being temporarily interned in a church behind the lines during World War II. This one-act play is concerned with the experience of these four men during a single night of internment, with the nervous tensions involved as they come to grips with grim reality. What distinguishes *A Sleep of Prisoners,* however, is not the psychological analysis of these tensions, but the presentation of the dramatist's insight into the significance of seemingly common situations among prisoners.

The action of the play revolves around the dilemma of modern man, the conflict between antinomies as represented by Privates David King and Peter Able: "between commitment and detachment, action and passivity—but also and simultaneously the conflict between the basic opposites which confront man perennially—between the claims of time and eternity, body and soul, the way of affirmation and nega-tion."[34] To David King who stands for the active force, Peter Able's indifference to their situation is simply unbearable. The calmness of this "no-complaint Pete" throws David into a rage, precipitating him into an attempt to throttle the other. Corporal Adams parts the two, and drags David to his bunk. In the sleep that follows, however, the agony is developed by the two dreams in which David, first as Cain, expresses the hedonistic view, and Able the idealistic. In the first dream, the violence David resorts to is bestial; in the second dream, the destructive force is reasoned: Private David as King of Israel orders the slaying of his son, Absalom (represented by Peter Able), for political expedience. The movement is from a beastly to a reasoned violence, both ending in the destruction of the passive character. These two dreams make up the *agon* or the first part of the play. The conflict developed in this first part is resolved in the second, consisting of the dreams of sacrifice and suffering. To redeem men from the intricate web of their passionate conflicts, God chose a people. To test the faith of Abraham from whose race the Redeemer would be born, God ordered the sacrifice of Isaac, Abraham's only son. The third dream in *A Sleep of Prisoners* is Peter Able's speaking as Isaac, with David King as Abraham. Again the role of the slayer is David's,

---

[34] William V. Spanos, " 'A Sleep of Prisoners': The Choreography of Comedy," *Modern Drama,* VIII (May 1965), 64.

and that of the victim is Able's. It is Corporal Adams who speaks as the angel informing Abraham that it is God's will that Isaac should live.

The play ends with the fourth dream whose fabric is as mixed up and incongruous as the stuff that dreams are often made of. It is Corporal Adams who dreams that he is on a raft floating on the ocean. When he has been joined by David and Peter, their talk reverts to their situation as prisoners, and proceeds to a biblical situation suggested by the name Nebuchadnezzar which Peter utters. And they feel that they are the men in the fiery furnace (Book of Daniel): Shadrac, Meshac, Abednego. Peter notices a fourth figure watching them through the flames. Announcing himself as "Man under God's command," Tim Meadows assures them that they would be able to come through if they have "The patience and the love...the honesty,/And quick eyes to see where evil is." It is Peter who declares that in the fiery furnace that engulfs them,

> The flames are men: all human...
> Breath and blood chokes and burns us.

But he adds:

> This
> Surely is unquenchable? It can only transform.
> There's no way out. We can only stay and alter.

This is the solution which is being offered to modern man's dilemma— that there is no escape from suffering, but if we let it, it will transform us. Meadows as the fourth figure becomes the raissoneur of the play. "The human heart can go to lengths of God," he asserts.

After integrating four outstanding events of the Old Testament into the play, the dramatist projects the New Testament in the fourth figure of the last dream. In the first of the sequences dramatizing the consequences of the Fall of Man as conflict among the sons of Adam, the voice of Jehovah had been spoken by Tim Meadows. At the end of the play, the epithets used by Adams and David suggest that Meadows now appears in the figure of Christ. "You cockeyed son of heaven, how did you get here?" cries Adams. "...the crowing son of heaven/Thinks we can make a morning," David exclaims cynically. And Tim Meadows ends the dream by summarizing the plight of men:

> The frozen misery
> Of centuries breaks, begins to move;
> The thunder is the thunder of the floes,
> The thaw, the flood, the upstart of Spring.
> Thank God our time is now when wrong
> Comes up to face us everywhere,
> Never to leave us till we take
> The longest stride of soul men ever took.
> Affairs are now soul size.
> The enterprise
> Is exploration into God. (p. 49)

This also sums up the night of these prisoners. It was a night which would lead to a morning brightened by the dawn of meaning. And the end strikes a note vastly different from that struck at the commencement of the play. The prisoners try to go to sleep once more.

> "Well, sleep, I suppose," says Adams.
> "Yeh. God bless," replies David.
> "Rest you merry" is Peter's wish.

The final chord is Tim Meadows' "Hope so. Hope so." There is a note of calm, as of conflict resolved. Morning finds the prisoners at rest after a night of restless dreaming. And we somehow feel that the dramatist is hinting at the morning that will also come after the troubled night of our times, even if

> It takes
> So many thousand years to wake, ... (p. 49)

Fry has so to speak immortalized the sleep of four prisoners in a play dramatizing the story of the human race through the impersonation of biblical figures with which the soldiers identify themselves in their dreams. By switching from the dramaturgy he followed in *The Firstborn* to the intricate machinery of *A Sleep of Prisoners,* the dramatist gives evidence of the tendency in contemporary drama to project action in the present as "re-enactment of the archetype that recurs over and over again."[35] This technique which Auerback calls figural is identical with what T. S. Eliot has termed the mythical method, the manipulating of "a continuous parallel between contem-

---

35 *Ibid.,* p. 72.

poraneity and antiquity."[36] It is also the method which Joyce pursued in Ulysses. The effect of this technique is the illumination which makes it attain universal significance while retaining the presentness of its identity.[37]

The night of conflict and pain which the four prisoners experience is "but a shadow of our history stealing across the sky."[38] And in these men suffering during World War II, we perceive the nightmare of the ages re-enacted in the dreams of a night. The mystery of human suffering that has baffled men of the Bible is once more grappled with by these four men imprisoned in a church. And just as the darkness of the race changes into light at Christmas, the night of these prisoners passes away with the advent of the Christ figure announcing the morning of hope.

---

[36] T.S. Eliot, "Ulysses, Order, and Myth," *Dial,* lxxv (November 1923), 480-83.

[37] See Spanos, *loc. cit.*

[38] Cf. lines said by David King in *A Sleep of Prisoners,* p. 31.

CHAPTER THREE

Two Types of Dramaturgy

The experiments of dramatists with biblical themes may give one the impression of being confronted by a motley legion. However, it seems possible to discern in the variety, two main types of dramaturgy which are determined by the dramatist's method of approaching his audience. As one of the aims of representation on the stage is to amuse, it is only natural that the author should consider the character of the audience whom his play is to amuse, and what kind of amusement he should offer to them.[1] Even when the aim is to pose or to answer some question, it is highly important that the dramatist be able to sustain the interest of his audience for a definite length of time, if his play is to succeed.

Today's dramatists are keenly aware of the obvious hiatus between them and their audience, as well as between members of the audience themselves. It is, therefore, essential that a common ground be found, whether it be moral, intellectual or emotional, on which the artist may meet the group of people for whom he is writing his play.[2]

In taking up a biblical theme, the dramatist may possibly assume one or other of two attitudes. First, he may consider his audience to be skeptical regarding material from the Bible. An effective way of holding the attention of such an audience in regard to a biblical subject might be to invite it to re-analyze the material, re-evaluate the old interpretations, consider reasons pro and con, and even to draw

---

[1] Cf. T.S. Eliot, *Selected Essays* (London: Faber and Faber Ltd., 1963), p. 45.

[2] Sean Lucy, *T. S. Eliot and the Idea of Tradition* (London: Cohen & West, 1967), p. 173.

some conclusion. This is the method followed by Jean Giraudoux in *Judith* as well as in *Cantique de Cantiques.* To an audience that finds it difficult to understand how a beautiful woman can keep her chastity in the circumstances in which Judith had found herself, Jean Giraudoux proposes what to him seems to be a plausible interpretation. The changing psychological conditions of the heroine are analyzed and portrayed in some kind of debate in which the dramatist presents two sides of the question as to whether Judith is the saint who has been venerated in the Old Testament. So is *Cantique de Cantiques* a discussion enriched by poetic echoes from its biblical counterpart, for in their conversation, Florence and Monsieur le President bring out various aspects in the love of a young woman for the old one as well as for the young lover. In this play, too, Giraudoux suggests a matter-of-fact explanation as substitute for the poetic situation of the original. The conclusion he leads his audience to, as a result of discussions he subtly interweaves in the dialogues, is that there is nothing spiritual in the changing psychology of a woman— this can be explained as physiological necessity: an interpretation which can capture any audience on the grounds of mere "common sense." In *Back to Methuselah,* Shaw goes further: he not only makes the characters discuss the plausibility of his pet theory of the Life Force, he also devotes two parts to elaborate exemplifications of what would happen if people made use of the power latent in them.

The second way of approaching the audience might be to assume a common belief in the truth of the Bible. The dramatist would then proceed to project his vision of this truth in the concrete, sharing it with his audience as intimately as he knows how. This has been done in varying degrees of intensity and from diverse points of view in the rest of the plays considered so far, from *Nobodaddy* to *A Sleep of Prisoners.* In all these plays, with the exception of *Lazarus Laughed,* the dramatist does not take any traditional Scriptural interpretation to task. He starts, so to speak, with the assumption that his audience is aware of the biblical original and can at least sympathize with the characters' motives in their respective situations. *Lazarus Laughed* is a play apart, in that the intellectual discussion does not take place in the play itself, but is implied by the interpretation given to the character of Lazarus, which is presumed by the dramatist and felt by the audience. The questions, "Was Lazarus truly a disciple of Christ? What happened after his rising from the dead?" have been answered indirectly by the dramatist in *Lazarus Laughed*. But in answering these, he assumes that the feelings of the audience, at least during the performance, will be caught in the atmosphere created, and thus, in spite of themselves, they will follow the dramatist's own vision of Lazarus.

To illustrate in greater detail these divergent methods of dramaturgy, the presentation of an intellectual discussion and the sharing of a dramatic vision, I should like to consider two plays in both of which biblical themes are integrated into action, one contemporary, the other historical.

PRESENTING AN INTELLECTUAL DISCUSSION —ARCHIBALD MACLEISH'S *J. B.*

We shall consider one of the most controversial pieces in modern American drama—Archibald MacLeish's *J. B.,* representing the first method of audience-approach through intellectual discussion. A New England writer whose career has included the roles of editor, statesman and Harvard professor,[3] MacLeish began his work as a playwright with *Nobodaddy* in 1925. The seven other plays [4] he has written since then show a movement from modified Greek classicism, through symbolism, to the Brechtian epic theatre which favors the method of intellectual discussion.

Completed in 1956, *J. B.* caught the attention of the theatrical world for the first time in 1958 when it was brought by Yale to the Brussels World Fair. It then came to New York in the winter and "was immediately generated into a sort of theatrical thunderbolt that strikes about once in a decade."[5] But the public's reaction developed into something like a hornet's nest, with a volley of divergent opinions coming from the most eminent dramatic critics of the country. Brooks

---

[3] MacLeish was editor of *Fortune* magazine from 1929 to 1938; he held various posts in the government: Director of the Office of Facts and Figures in 1941, Assistant Director of the Office of War Information, 1942-43, Assistant Secretary of State, 1944-45, Chairman of the American Delegation to the London Conference of the United Nations to establish a Cultural and Educational Organization in 1945, and Harvard professor from 1949 to the time of his retirement in 1962 when he was seventy.

[4] *Panic, The Fall of the City, Air Raid, The Trojan Horse, This Music Crept by Me upon the Waters, J. B., Herakles.* Of these, the second, third, fourth and fifth are radio plays. (Cited in letter to the author dated April 5, 1965.)

[5] *Newsweek,* December 22, 1958, p. 45.

Atkinson of *The New York Times* is said to have called *J. B.* one of the memorable works of the century.[6] From Joseph Wood Krutch we have the following comment:

> This is indeed the most impressive play among those even remotely similar in method or intention that I have met in many years.[7]

However, the other side holds as many weighty opinions. Henry Hewes of *The Saturday Review* dubs it a "stillborn classic."[8] *The New Yorker*'s Kenneth Tynan thinks that "the ending cheats."[9] Tom Driver of *The Christian Century* explains why the ending causes disappointment:

> He has begun by raising the most searching questions regarding the relationship of God and man. Yet he has ended by asserting that man is himself the answer to these questions, which is as much to say that the religious questions were false to begin with.[10]

To Irving Feldman, the defect in *J. B.* "is not a result of MacLeish's imperfect stagecraft, but derives from his vision of the world."[11]

The amount of criticism elicited for and against *J. B.* only goes to prove that it is indeed one of the most controversial plays ever presented on the American stage. Whether or not *J. B.* becomes one of the lasting achievements of art and mind in our times, it will remain one of the remarkable dramas of our century.

The Biblical Theme in *J. B.*

Like Giraudoux's plot in *Judith*, *J. B.*'s runs in a movement parallel to the biblical account, this time the *Book of Job*. MacLeish's modern Job is the New England banker, J. B., a millionaire with a beautiful wife and five lovely children. Just like Job, the New England banker loses his children one by one; his wealth disappears in an explosion, apparently of an atom bomb, as an effect of which his skin is afflicted with sores. All through these incidents, he repeats Job's words:

---

6 "First-Nighters Cheered," *ibid.*
7 "The Universe at Stage Center," *Theatre Arts*, August 1958, pp. 9-11.
8 May 10, 1958.
9 December 20, 1958.
10 June 11, 1958.
11 *Commentary*, August 1958, p. 183.

> The Lord giveth. . .
> The Lord taketh away!
> Blessed be the name of the Lord.

In the bitterest of invectives, his wife, Sarah, accuses God of killing her children who were innocent. She bids J. B. curse God and die. Not succeeding in persuading him, Sarah departs, and, as she confesses later, is tempted to throw herself into the river to end it all. On the stairs, however, she finds a forsythia blooming among the ashes. And she cannot find it in herself to end her life. She goes back to J. B. who notices that his skin is clean. To his question, "Why did you leave me alone?" she answers:

>   I loved you.
> I couldn't help you any more.
> You wanted justice and there was none—
> Only love.

So far, there is no remarkable departure from the biblical original. But J. B.'s next words come with the impact of a shock:

> He does not love. He is.

This line should be considered in conjunction with the lines spoken by Nickles in the Prologue:

> If God is God He is not good,
> If God is good He is not God.

Goodness and love go together. To say that God loves would be tantamount to saying that He is good. MacLeish, in the mouth of both Nickles and J. B., obviously denies God's goodness and His love. It is possible that MacLeish means that God's goodness cannot be measured by human terms. In his dialogues with Van Doren, we come across the following passages which reiterate the idea that "God is not good."

> Van Doren: Incidentally, in *J. B.*—this is just a parenthesis—in *J. B.*
>   I remember being terribly hard hit both in reading the play and in
>   seeing it, by two lines that Nickles, I guess, says: "If God is God,
>   He is not good: if God is good, He is not God." Were they early?
> MacLeish: Yes, they were early.
> Van Doren: Well, I'm so glad they are there, because that's the whole
>   point, isn't it, about God?

MacLeish: That little song was always there as Nickles uses it in describing Job's situation.

Van Doren: Yes, but you see, what you've got hold of there is the essence of Job, because Job is about the fact that God is not good. God is God.

MacLeish: Yes.

Van Doren: I suppose the simplest fact about God, if I may be presumptuous, is that He's not a good man, He's not a man at all. Is that right? God is not a man; He's God. His power is His attribute, not his goodness.

MacLeish: Exactly, and this is what the whole Book of Job is about.

Van Doren: Of course it's about that. And, by the way, all myths honor this distinction. I mean, the Greek myths do, too.

MacLeish: What happens when God appears in a cloud of dust and silences Job? He silences him not by proving to Job that Job is wrong, but by proving to Job that God is powerful and Job isn't. "Where wast thou when I laid the foundations?"[12]

In the play, the conclusion that God is power rather than love, is reached by a wealthy New England banker who cannot conceive of suffering as an expression of love. Like the typical Puritan, he has expected God to give him prosperity, considering his blameless life. And so he is surprised when adversity falls on him. In his and Sarah's narrow vision, suffering can only be a punishment meted out for guilt. And so Sarah asks:

> Why did He do it to them?
> What had they done to Him—those children . . .
> What had they done to Him . . .
> > and we—
> What had *we* done? . . .
> > What had *we* done? (p. 70)

J. B.'s prayer shows that his thoughts do not turn to God as the all-wise Being whose plans are best though difficult to understand. Instead he concentrates on himself: "Show me my guilt, O God! . . . Show me my transgression," is his repeated cry. It is an obsession with the thought of guilt. To J. B.,

> Guilt matters. Guilt must always matter.
> Unless guilt matters the whole world is
> Meaningless. (p. 122)

---

12 Warren V. Bush, *The Dialogues of Archibald MacLeish and Mark Van Doren* (New York: Dutton & Co., 1964), pp. 138-39.

Nonetheless, he does not accept Zophar's statement that his sin consists in his being born a man. To think that man's heart is evil, that his fault, his sin is heart and will, is to make the Creator of the universe "the miscreator of mankind— a party to the crimes He punishes..." (p. 126). J. B. still believes in God:

> God is God or we are nothing—

But it is no longer the God in whom the Job of the Old Testament had trusted. Sarah never denies the existence of God. Yet she no longer sees how God does enter into their lives. She notices the forsythia blooming among the ashes, but it does not make her think that faith in God can survive with the tender bloom of love after human suffering. She cannot see the relationship between suffering and the design of Providence.

The faith of J. B. and Sarah has, so to speak, become faithless. They believe that God exists, but they think Him to be indifferent to their sufferings. And so they leave Him to Himself, and go their way "to blow on the coal of the heart," hoping that by their own efforts, by their own light, they may be able to see by and by, and to know the meaning of human suffering. It is a version different from the biblical narrative of the man of Hus who could learn from nature that "A tree hath hope. If it be cut, it groweth green again, and the boughs thereof sprout;" (Job 14:7). Job could say in suffering:

> . . . I know that my Redeemer liveth, and in the last day I shall rise out of the earth.
>   And I shall be clothed again with my skin; and in my flesh I shall see my God,
>   Whom I myself shall see and my eyes shall behold; and not another. This my hope is laid up in my bosom. (Job 19:25-27)

At the core of both *J. B.* and the *Book of Job* is the problem of human suffering. J. B. suffers and can only think of suffering as a punishment for guilt. Not being aware of any guilt, he concludes that in making him suffer, God does not love him—does not love man. To him, God's existence is something apart. But men can bear this suffering that He gives, because they can love one another. To Job of the Old Testament, suffering is the pledge of a future resurrection.

The question asked in both books is the same; in fact, it is that which men have asked through the ages: "Why does man suffer?"

The answer MacLeish gives is not the biblical answer: MacLeish does not justify God's ways to men but rather men's ways to God. Men suffer in London, Dresden, Hiroshima by the thousands, he says, "for sleeping the wrong night in the wrong city." Their suffering is meaningless, but they manage to bear it because they love one another. This is the message that MacLeish conveys through *J. B.* It is an answer which somehow evades the question. For it does not tell us for what purpose men suffer; it merely explains how they can live in spite of suffering. Is MacLeish's message but one more statement of what Eliot had given us in *The Waste Land,* that men today do not know the meaning of suffering, their spirit being too barren to cultivate thoughts about the designs of God in human life?

In the ending of *J. B.,* however, there is a message of hope symbolized by the forsythia: In this wasteland, there is still the bloom of life giving promise of a brighter future. And so man looks forward to the time when the light from the coal of the heart may enable him to see the meaning of human suffering. This is doubtful, though, for suffering can only have its fullness of meaning in the world of faith— which is on a supernatural plane. The light that J. B. speaks of remains on the human level. With nothing but the human, is it possible to reach the meaning of the divine plan? And so, the humanism of MacLeish fails to answer the theological question posed by *J. B.* in a way that the Old Testament's ardent faith expressed in the *Book of Job* can.

What we may call the biblical theme in *J. B.* is simply the motif of the just man whom God tries by means of a series of adversities. The strain of thought conveyed by the play, however, is nonbiblical, for J. B. and Sarah conclude in the last scene that the God who gives sufferings is loveless, but that the human sufferers, by loving one another, render themselves capable of bearing the burden of life. In the mystery of human suffering, in the incomprehensibility of God's ways with man, the biblical spirit is expressed in Psalm XXI:

> O God, my God, look upon me: Why hast thou forsaken me? . . .
> O my God, I shall cry by day and thou wilt not hear: and by night, and it shall not be reputed as folly in me.
> But thou dwellest in the holy place, the praise of Israel.

> In thee have our fathers hoped: they have hoped,
> and thou hast delivered them.
> They cried to thee, and they were saved: they
> trusted in thee, and were not confounded.
> But I am a worm and no man; the reproach of men
> and the outcast of the people.[13]

Incapable of fathoming God's mind, the just man of the Bible acknowledges his limitations while strengthening his trust in God who had shown him and his fathers mercy and deliverance in the past. Whereas the acceptance of suffering in the Bible is based upon reliance on the Providence of God, that in *J. B.* is founded on confidence in the human ability to bear pain through love.

Conception and Execution in *J. B.*—the Discussion

Like many a masterpiece in literature, *J. B.* can be traced to a soul-racking experience leaving indelible traces in the author. What ideas MacLeish conveyed in *J. B.* arise from an event which, though not directly related to his personal life, left in him an impression so deep as to stir his thoughts and prompt him to write one of his major pieces.

In the dialogues with Van Doren previously mentioned, MacLeish shares with us the situation which gave impulse to the composition of his play.

> . . . Just after the Battle of Britain, I went down to West Ham, down the Thames River, below London, east of London, and the thing that was so overwhelming was not the thousands of destroyed houses, the thing that was overwhelming was the people, most of them Scots people . . . and all of them bewildered and entirely innocent victims of Nazi bombing. They got bombed because the curve of the river there made a mark that the bombers could see on a moonlight night as they came over. That was their sin; they lived in a place where the moon shone on the river. And that, and the fact that you found family after family which, bombed out here, had gone to the west of London and been bombed out there. One family had gone way up to the north of the country and by chance had been bombed out there. There were two of them left out of eight.

---

[13] Douai-Rheims

> Well, this sort of thing makes a sort of pattern of meaninglessness, and to deal with meaninglessness, to deal with tragic meaninglessness, meant to find a metaphor and here was the metaphor, the Book of Job.[14]

Seeing the plight of evacuees, their apparently undeserved suffering, MacLeish saw in this a pattern of meaninglessness. And as the poet wondered how he could write about this "in terms of essence," he hit upon the figure of Job who is, according to Mark Van Doren, "the very symbol of suffering, undeserved suffering, suffering which nobody can understand."[15]

What MacLeish wanted to produce, therefore, was not a historical play based on Job. It was modern man that intrigued him—Job in a twentieth-century situation. The very title, *J. B.*, attempts to give a modern touch to an old name. Having found the prototype for the suffering man, the playwright proceeded to paraphrase the old narrative in terms of our modern world. The counterpart of the wealthy man of Hus is a New England banker. Instead of the sheep and cattle of the former, we have the millions of dollars lost by the modern man. And the fire which consumes these is the atom bomb. Unlike the children of Job, those of J. B. die separately, except for the two who die together in an automobile crash.

The variety in the messengers ranging from the drunken policeman to the callous cameraman is an attempt to make the whole picture unmistakably up-to-date and as colorful as the modern world can be. The comforters of J. B.—the determinist, the spoiled cleric and psychiatrist—present a parody of their biblical counterparts.

In a study of the plot of *J. B.*, we find that the first noticeable departure from the *Book of Job* consists in the change of emphasis in the incidents. Where the Old Testament book limits the treatment of calamities befalling Job to two chapters out of fifty-two, MacLeish devotes more than half of the action in his play to the announcements of the deaths of J. B.'s children and the loss of his property. On the other hand, the comforters who are given a major part in the *Book of Job* are relegated to just one scene in *J. B.* There is no character in *J. B.* corresponding to the Eliu of the Old Testament narrative.

The essentially distinguishing feature in the dramaturgy of *J. B.*, however, lies in the presentation of the conflict between the power of

---

[14] Warren V. Bush, *op. cit.*, pp. 105-06.
[15] *Ibid.*

good and the power of evil, a theme which is contiguous with the problem of human suffering. In the *Book of Job*, God Himself speaks, and so does the devil. Now, reckoning with the sophistication of a twentieth-century audience, MacLeish knew that it would not do to make a presentation similar to the medieval mystery play. MacLeish knew that it would be difficult to get a Broadway audience to witness a modern play with God the Father and the Devil in the cast. He therefore came upon the idea of a sort of rambling debate between the forces of good and of evil. This debate is held by two ham actors, Mr. Zuss who wears the God-mask, and Nickles who wears the Satan-mask. MacLeish avows that he was "bogged down" until he conceived of Mr. Zuss and Nickles as a pair of circus hangers-on.[16] Now, the lines of the God-mask and the Satan-mask are taken word for word from the Bible. What keeps the play moving, however, is not these biblical quotations, but the comments of Mr. Zuss without the God-mask, and still more of Nickles without the Satan-mask. For in MacLeish's presentation, the thoughts and sentiments of these circus hangers-on are in keeping with the lines they recite when wearing their masks. The dialogues between Mr. Zuss and Nickles have a major role in the play. Remove these discussions, and the play can no longer stand before its Broadway audience. These dialogues are an extremely ingenious device used by MacLeish to arouse suspense in a play where the ending is known from the very start. They focus the attention on the action which consists in the changes that take place in the mind of J. B. The comments of Nickles, in particular, have the effect of making us feel that the ancient notion of the patient man as portrayed by the Bible is being challenged. When he says in Scene Two,

> Shall I tell you how it ends?
> Shall I prophesy? I see our
> Smug world-master on his dung heap,
> Naked, miserable, and alone,
> Pissing the stars. Ridiculous gesture!—
> Nevertheless a gesture—meaning
> All there is on earth to mean:
> Man's last word . . . and worthy of him!

the audience wonder whether the modern Job will act as his biblical counterpart had done. Listening to Mr. Zuss and Nickles, the audience

---

16 *Ibid.*, pp. 137-38.

are, so to speak, rooted to their seats: the boredom of looking at something they already know is removed, and they begin to identify themselves either with one or the other point of view, so that the dialogue between these characters representing the forces of good and of evil gradually becomes a discussion full of verve, echoing their own intellectual processes. The conservative find their thoughts expressed in the lines of Mr. Zuss; the cynical recognize their sentiments only too eloquently conveyed by Nickles, who evidently has the upper hand.

It was Shaw who claimed that "discussion" is the characteristic of modern drama. In *The Quintessence of Ibsenism,* Shaw explained, "Formerly you had in what was called a well-made play an exposition in the first act, a situation in the second, and unravelling in the third. Now you have exposition, situation, and discussion; and the discussion is the test of the playwright."[17] He was describing Ibsen's technique as well as his own in plays where a kind of discussion provides the solution to the problem that had been created in the conflict. According to John Gassner, " 'Discussion' should be equated with the manifestation of a critical spirit that helps to shape the modern realistic play and give it a significance well above that of merely pictorial realism."[18]

As MacLeish uses it in *J. B.*, discussion precedes and inter-penetrates the action, as the following outline of the play will demonstrate.

J. B.

STATEMENT AND DISCUSSION	ACTION
<div align="center">PROLOGUE</div>	

Three Statements
   made by Nickles, now and
   then reproved by Mr. Zuss,
   at times approved:
1. If God is God
     He is not good,
  If God is good
     He is not God. (p. 11)

---

[17] Bernard Shaw, *Major Critical Essays: 'The Quintessence of Ibsenism,' 'The Perfect Wagnerite,' 'The Sanity of Art'* (London: Constable and Co. 1955 reprint), p. 135.

[18] *Form and Idea in Modern Theatre* (New York: The Dryden Press, 1956), pp. 41-42.

STATEMENT AND DISCUSSION   ACTION

2. Job is everywhere we go,
   His children dead, his
       work for nothing,
   Counting his losses,
       scraping his boils,
   Discussing himself with his
       friends and physicians
   Questioning everything—
       the times, the stars,
   His own soul, God's
       providence. (p. 13)
3. Justice[19] has a face
      like this . . .
      (Indicates the mask)
      Of stone. (p. 17)

SCENE ONE

SITUATION from which the action starts:
The family of J. B. is shown as an
ideal New England family: free from
suffering. Sarah declares that this
good fortune is a reward to J. B.

SCENE TWO

(Nickles and Mr. Zuss comment on
J. B.'s acting.)
Nickles' STATEMENT:
   A rich man's piety stinks
   You know what talks when that
              man's talking?
   All that gravy on his plate—
   His cash—his pretty wife—
            his children!
   Lift the lot of them, he'd sing
   Another canticle to different music.
              (p. 46)
Mr. Zuss' ANSWER:
   God will show him what God is—
   Enormous pattern of the steep
            of stars . . . (p. 47)
   Nothing this good man might
          suffer,

---

[19] Justice is here equated with God. The implication is that God's justice is
cold and unfeeling.

STATEMENT AND DISCUSSION   ACTION

Nothing at all, would make him
      yelp
As you do. He'd praise God
      no matter. (p. 48)
Nickles' QUESTION:
  Why must he suffer then?
Mr. Zuss: To praise. To see God.
Nickles' PROPHECY:
  I see our
Smug world-master on his dung
      heap,
Naked, miserable, and alone;
Pissing the stars. Ridiculous
      gesture!—
Nevertheless a gesture—meaning
All there is on earth to mean:
Man's last word . . . and
      worthy of him! (p. 49)
Mr. Zuss' PROPHECY:
  This man will not. He trusts
      God.
No matter how it ends, he trusts
      Him.

SCENE THREE

  * Two soldiers come to inform J. B.
    and Sarah of the death of their
    eldest son, David, through a mistaken
    order in the army.
  * The Reaction:
    J. B.'s cry: It isn't
      True you little drunken liar!
      It can't be true. It isn't
          possible. (p. 60)
    Sarah's cry:
      David is our son, our son,
          our son. (p. 61)

SCENE FOUR

  * Messengers announce the death of
    J. B.'s two children, Mary and Jon-
    athan in a car accident.
  * The Reaction:
    J. B.'s answer:
      We have to take the chances,
          Sarah;

STATEMENT AND DISCUSSION   ACTION

Evil with good.
It doesn't mean there
Is no good.
Sarah's reply:
When you were lucky it
                was God! (p. 71)

SCENE FIVE

Mr. Zuss and Nickles discuss J. B.'s
inability to act.
Nickles' STATEMENT:
He doesn't have to act.
    He suffers.
It's an old role—played like a
    mouth-organ. (Sarcastic)
                (p. 75)

* The two messengers announce the
death of J. B.'s youngest girl, Rebecca, raped by a maniac.
The Reaction: Recognition of the trial
    by J. B. who says,
        The Lord giveth,
            the Lord taketh away.
                (p. 83)

SCENE SIX

* Two messengers enter, carrying Sarah between them, to announce the
death of J. B.'s daughter, Ruth, at
an explosion that reduced the whole
of his bank to debris.
The Reaction:
J. B.'s resignation:
    The Lord giveth.
    The Lord taketh away . . .
                (p. 89)
Blessed be the name of
    the Lord. (p. 90)
Sarah's rebellion:
                Takes!
    Kills! Kills! Kills! Kills!
                (p. 89)

SCENE SEVEN

Reactions to J. B.'s
acceptance of God's Will:

STATEMENT AND DISCUSSION	ACTION

Mr. Zuss: I think that great
Yea-saying to the world
  was wonderful—
That wounded and deliberate
  Amen—
That—affirmation. (p. 92)

Nickles: . . . I think it stinks
One daughter raped and mur-
  dered by an idiot,
Another crushed by stones,
  a son
Destroyed by some fool
  officer's stupidity,
Two children smeared across
  a road
At midnight by a drunken
  child—
And all with God's consent—
  foreknowledge!
And he blesses God!
. . . It's disgusting! (p. 93)

The Question and Its Answer:

Mr. Zuss: Would Job be better
  off asleep
Among the clods of earth in
  ignorance?

Nickles: Yes, when he suffers
  in his body;
Yes, when his suffering is
  him.

Statements:

Mr. Zuss: His suffering will
  praise.

Nickles: It will not.

SCENE EIGHT

Nickles and a chorus of women
  recall the situation of
  suffering for J. B. and Sarah.
Action in the hour of suffering:
  1. J. B. is baffled by the apparent
    meaninglessness of suffering but
    reasserts
      (a) the justice of God
      (b) and his own guilt,

STATEMENT AND DISCUSSION

ACTION

2. Sarah says that we have the choice to live or die.
3. She leaves J. B.

SCENE NINE

The chorus of women describes the Three Comforters who enter the scene.

The Three Comforters try to convince J. B. with their arguments.

Discussion of guilt by
the Three Comforters:
Bildad, the Marxist, explains guilt as a sociological accident.
Zophar, the spoiled priest, declares that one's sin consists in being born a man.
Eliphaz, the psychiatrist, reduces sin to a psychological phenomenal situation.

J. B. refuses to disown his guilt by explaining it away as the comforters have done.

SCENE TEN

Nickles and Mr. Zuss describe J. B.'s spiritless reaction to misfortune:
Nickles likens him to "goddam sheep without the spunk to spit on Christmas!" (p. 136)
Mr. Zuss is disappointed, for J. B.'s "giving in" was not in a spirit of praising God but rather in an attitude of forgiving Him.

Nickles suggests suicide to J. B. as a rejection of suffering coming from God.

The approach of someone prevents J. B. from considering the suggestion deeply.

SCENE ELEVEN

Sarah returns to J. B.

She confesses that her intention to drown herself in the river was prevented by the discovery of a forsythia blooming among the ashes.

J. B. reproves her for having told him
to curse God and die, and for leaving
him.

She explains that it was because she
could not help him anymore, inasmuch as he wanted justice, and there
was no justice but only love.

J. B. declares that
"He (God) does not love.
He is." (p. 152)

Sarah reminds him that even if He
does not love, they do. She admon-
ishes him to "blow on the coal of
the heart," since "The candles in
churches are out." (p. 153)

Thus loving each other, they think
that someday, they would know...

In the prologue, the revolutionary hypothesis about God not
being good places the audience on its guard, arming itself with the
critical spirit with which to evaluate this and similar forthright statements in the play. The second declaration made is that "Job is everywhere we go," which is to say that J. B. is not really just an individual,
nor is he the biblical hero, but a kind of representative of suffering
men. The third assertion implies that suffering is a result of God's
justice, and that He inflicts it without sympathy for the victim. These
statements demand argument which is provided for in the play.

The first scene sketches the situation of the successful New England
banker on whose side God seems to have always been. This makes us
ready for the next remark of Nickles in Scene Two that if this good
fortune were lifted from him, J. B., the rich man, would behave differ-
ently. The contrary is asserted by Mr. Zuss who claims that no matter
what happens, J. B. will trust in God.

We have the actual demonstration in Scenes Three, Four and
Five, in which messengers come to report the death of J. B.'s children;
in Scene Six in which he is informed of the loss of all his wealth along
with the death of his last daughter; and in Scene Eight in which we
see him covered with sores. There is a kind of parenthetical discussion
of guilt in Scene Nine, since J. B. has all the while considered suffering
as a punishment. The three explanations of guilt have evidently been
picked out as representative of various points of view opposed to the

orthodox Christian idea of sin: the Communist's, the fallen Christian's, and the psychiatrist's.

The question of the meaning of suffering has been taken up in Scene Two, Mr. Zuss declaring that pain serves for praise and for enabling man to see God. And now that J. B.'s faith has been found to be unshaken, the argument takes another turn. Granted that J. B.'s attitude in suffering is an acceptance of God's will, the next question raised (in Scene Ten) is whether such affirmation is the manly reaction. Nickles considers rejection of suffering through suicide as indicative of the human power to assert itself.

The conclusion of the play contains MacLeish's answer: The solution to the problem of human suffering is not suicide but love. God's ways may be incomprehensible, but men have an unfailing resource—the capability to love which may finally enable them not only to bear but perhaps also to understand, someday, the mystery of human suffering.

By interweaving argumentative dialogue and action, MacLeish has succeeded in presenting discussions of such questions as the meaning of human suffering, man's attitude toward pain, and the means of bearing it. The method is predominantly intellectual, and the effect aimed at is a quickening of the spectator's critical faculty, making it probe further into questions whose answers given previously seem to conflict with experience.

J. B. as Epic Theatre

As MacLeish himself had avowed, his play was bogged down until he conceived the device of utilizing two characters who are not really involved in the action being presented. The moment he decided on including the circus hangers-on, Mr. Zuss and Nickles, to recite the lines for the God-mask and the Satan-mask, as well as to make comments, the poet had determined his dramaturgy in favor of epic theatre.

Among the writers of our age, few are as well read as MacLeish. He has access to Spanish and German literatures in the original, not to mention French in which he is as much at home as in English.[20] He could not be ignorant of the German dramatist and his theory of

---

[20] In a letter to the author dated April 5, 1965.

epic theatre. Even should MacLeish's reading of Brecht's works be limited, he has surely noticed the development of the epic theatre in American drama, notably in Thornton Wilder. Besides this, MacLeish's readings of French drama could not have excluded the plays of Paul Claudel who also developed an epic theatre based on his observation of Chinese and Japanese drama. There is something, for instance, in the dramatic debate between Mr. Zuss and Nickles which recalls parts of Claudel's *Christophe Colomb* where the Explicateur and members of the chorus engage in a sort of verbal skirmish.[21]

A study of the technique used in *J. B.* will show that it possesses the main characteristics of the epic theatre as expounded by Bertolt Brecht.[22] For convenience, we shall take up these characteristics in regard to (1) the presentation of action; (2) the presentation of character; (3) the attitude expected of the audience; and (4) the actual effect on the audience.

Brecht's declaration, "Modern theatre is Epic theatre," is an assumption that the tendency in present-day playwrighting is to move away from the old dramatic form of theatre. Now, the term "Epic theatre" as used by Brecht denotes narrative as opposed to dramatic theatre. Epic theatre presents action not solely as taking place before the eyes of the spectator, but also as being narrated either by certain characters in the play or by extraneous personages in the form of commentators or their counterparts. In *J. B.*, the only action that takes place before the spectators can be reduced to the following: his refusal to curse God after his first losses, his wife's departure just in his moment of deepest desolation, the coming of the comforters, and the wife's return to J. B. The play's other incidents—the death of their

---

21 Cf. Part II, Scene 2, Paul Claudel: *Theatre II* (France, Editions Gallimard, 1956), pp. 1175-77.
22 The main differences between the old dramatic form of theatre and the epic form of theatre are shown below as quoted by John Willett in *The Theatre of Bertolt Brecht* (London: Methuen, 1959), p. 172:

DRAMATIC FORM OF THEATRE	EPIC FORM OF THEATRE
* Plot	* Narrative
* Implicates the spectator in a stage situation	* Turns the spectator into an observer, but
* Wears down his power of action	* Arouses his power of action
* The human being is taken for granted	* The human being is the object of inquiry
* He is unalterable	* He is alterable and able to alter
* Eyes on the finish	* Eyes on the course
* One scene makes another	* Each scene for itself
* Growth	* Montage

eldest son, David, by some mistaken order in the army; the death of their eldest daughter, Mary, and their younger boy, Jonathan, in an automobile crash; the assault on and murder of their youngest girl, Rebecca; the explosion that destroyed J. B.'s bank causing the death of their remaining daughter, Ruth—are all narrated by messengers. What the messengers do not narrate is left to Mr. Zuss, Nickles and the chorus of women. It is from Nickles at the beginning of Scene Eight that we come to know that the whole city had tumbled down and "one man's skin blisters with agony." The conversation of the women in the scene serves to accentuate the contrast between J. B. of the past and J. B. of the present. In the last scene devoted to Mr. Zuss and Nickles (Scene Ten), the words of the former are a comment, not on the action in the play but on the acting of J. B.— a criticism of his attitude (p. 135). MacLeish, therefore, has made extensive use of the narrator in the play.

Furthermore, if we study the incidents that make up the action in *J. B.,* we shall discover a great difference between this play and the plays in the classical tradition of Western drama. The European dramas based on a study of Aristotle's theory of tragedy are masterpieces of unity. The events are so selected and arranged that the causal connection is clear. Being an integral part of the whole, one event in the classical play cannot be removed without marring its organization. In *J. B.,* the incidents are so episodic in nature that the play can bear the removal of one or two scenes without any noticeable damage to the organization. The series of deaths announced to J. B. and Sarah are not essential to the catastrophe. They are not even arranged in the order of the greatness of grief that they would cause. They are, as Brecht had claimed for epic theatre, scenes that are separate each by itself. If they serve the play at all, it is only by their bringing out the details of adversity more vividly. They augment the weight of misfortune, so to speak, by their cumulative effect. In short, in *J. B.,* MacLeish employs the epic theatre device of *montage* by means of which one picture is placed beside another so that the sum of the pictures makes up the total story. The method is one of accumulation rather than of the growth that we find in the plot of classical drama.

In its presentation of man, *J. B.* is likewise epic theatre in tendency. According to Brecht, epic theatre should show man as a process, not as a being with fixed reactions. In this point, epic theatre is more immediately a reaction to naturalism which considers man as subject to scientific rules in his behavior. Remotely again, it is a departure from the classical idea that because of the common nature in men they generally act similarly under given conditions. Because of this knowledge of the human being both in his intellectual processes and in his passions, in the classical tragedy, the catastrophe had a certain inevitability. Now, in *J. B.*, man is shown as altering. MacLeish reveals the process by which the protagonist changes from the righteous and prosperous Puritan with a strong faith in God to one obviously disillusioned with Him and who finally considers Him as having no relationship to his life. If J. B. and Sarah are to bear their share of suffering in life, it is not, as their faith would have told them, with God's aid, but of their own human efforts to love. This is an ending which would have been difficult to foresee at the beginning of the play. Yet, MacLeish presents it as a plausible ending, apparently based on the same theory as Brecht's, namely, that man is not known; his reactions are therefore unpredictable. This was true of J. B. whose reiteration of the biblical lines is given the lie by his final statement: "He does not love. He is." For, whereas the lines from the *Book of Job* imply a trusting, loving submission to God, the concluding utterance of J. B. reveals the lack of any filial attitude toward God. Sarah's conduct, too, is unpredictable. It cannot be justified from the point of view of consistency. How she could leave J. B. alone in his misery and then come back to say the best lines on human love cannot be explained except by Brecht's statement that man is not known: man is a process, alterable and altering.

In listening to the arguments between Mr. Zuss and Nickles as commentators on the action presented in the play, the audience become aware of being only spectators of a play, not individuals involved in the action through sympathy with the characters. Whereas drama in the Aristotelian tradition effects a certain identification of the audience with the characters being presented, so as to produce a catharsis, epic theatre in the Brechtian theory aims at a *Verfremdung*—an alienation. The playwright, on purpose, attempts to make the spectator feel that he is a third person witnessing the acting, judging its merits, with his eye on the process of the presentation, not on the outcome of the plot. To produce this feeling in the audience, certain devices are resorted to. In *J. B.*, the dialogues between Mr. Zuss and Nickles discussing the reactions of the hero, and making comments on life, are evidently aimed at breaking the illusion of reality that might be created in the play. They "alienate" the audience so as to place them in a position to judge the story being presented, as objectively as possible. While watching the play, the audience are expected to judge the acting. They somehow know beforehand that J. B. will have a series of trials; they even have an idea how these will end. What they want to find out, therefore, is how he will take his situation, how he compares with his biblical archetype, and how well he corresponds to their empirical knowledge of modern man. Instead of producing a catharsis, J. B. is aimed at arousing an intellectual discussion similar to that between Mr. Zuss and Nickles. For the epic theatre does not intend to supply vicarious experience; its purpose is rather to stir the audience to a formulation of a view of the world.

Such a theatre expects an intellectual reaction from the audience, paving the way for action. According to Esslin, "The Brechtian theatre is a theatre designed to arouse indignation in the audience, dissatisfaction, a realization of contradiction—it is a theatre supremely fitted for parody, caricature, and denunciation, therefore essentially a negative theatre."[23] J. B. is, to a certain degree, a negation of certain theological tenets. Most striking is the statement: "He does not love. He is," which, as was pointed out previously, is virtually a denial of the Christian belief that God is love. MacLeish suggests that rather than being love, God is power. And the play makes use of discussion that somehow leads to this and related conclusions.

SHARING A DRAMATIC VISION—
PAUL CLAUDEL'S *L'ANNONCE FAITE À MARIE*

To illustrate the second method of audience approach, the sharing of a dramatic vision, I have chosen *L'Annonce Faite à Marie* written by the French dramatist, Paul Claudel, whose contribution to modern drama is now recognized not only in France but also in other countries where Christian themes can be appreciated in the theatre.

In Claudel's career as a dramatist, three periods are recognizable: (1) the period of the early dramas which are mainly autobiographical; (2) the period of the dramas with a historical background; (3) the

---

[23] Martin Esslin: *Brecht: The Man and His Work* (New York: Doubleday & Company, Inc., 1960), p. 153.

period of the masterpieces which embody his ideas of a Christian Cosmos.[24]

L'Annonce Faite à Marie was first conceived as *La Jeune Fille Violaine* in the first period of the dramatist's career, rewritten and given its present title during the second period, and finally endowed with its final shape during the third period. It may well be Claudel's favorite drama, as Wallace Fowlie has claimed, "The work he was most attached to, the one for which he expressed the most constant affection."[25] Although he wrote a second version of each of the early plays, with the exception of *Le Repos du Septième Jour*, it is only to the text of *L'Annonce* that he returned time and again, correcting and recorrecting it during a span of fifty-six years.

When *L'Annonce* was first played in Paris under the direction of Lugne Poe in the Théâtre de L'Oeuvre in 1912, reactions were mixed. Among those in the audience who were profoundly moved by the presentation was Paul Souday who recognized in the play a "veritable revelation."[26] There were many, however, whose prejudices against Claudel had built up a wall of indifference. Although presentations in Germany, in the United States and in various parts of the world had won the applause of admiring audiences, it was not till 1948, when the final version was presented at the Theatre Hebertot,

---

[24] The Dramas of Paul Claudel:

First Period: 1890-1905	Date of 2nd Version
1890: *Tête d'Or*	1894
La Ville	1897
1892: *La Jeune Fille Violaine*	1898
1893: *L'Échange*	1905
1896: *Le Repos du Septième Jour*	
1905: *Partage de Midi*	1948

Second Period: 1906-20
    1911: *L'Annonce faite à Marie*
    1913: *L'Otage*
    1918: *Le Pain Dur*
    1920: *Le Père Humilié*
Third Period: 1921-48
    1929: *Le Soulier de Satin*
    1933: *Le Livre de Christophe Colomb*
    1934: *Jeanne d'Arc au Bucher*
    1942: *L'Histoire de Tobie et de Sara*
    1948: *L'Annonce faite à Marie*
        (Final version for the stage)

[25] In the Introduction to *The Tidings Brought to Mary* (Chicago: Henry Regnery Co., 1960), p. vii.

[26] Louis Chaigne, *Vie de Paul Claudel et genese de son oeuvre* (France: Maison Mame, 1961), p. 124.

that the dramatist was at last satisfied with a performance of *L'Annonce*. The final homage to Claudel's dramatic genius would be paid seven years later when the Comedie-Française performed the play. The gala premiere, which took place on February 17, 1955, was presided over by none other than M. Rene Coty, President of France. It was time for the old poet to repeat the words he had said five years earlier: "A present, je puis mourir."[27] On the 24th of the same month, less than a week after the great event, death came to the poet. *L'Annonce* was his closing triumph.

When we study Claudel's dramas, we notice that where the auto-biographical strain is strong, generally there is a symbolism that accompanies the lyricism, transforming personal elements into material capable of being grasped by the audience. The poet has recourse to symbols to convey what cannot be adequately expressed in words, symbolism lending itself to the treatment of the subjective. Now, the subjective naturally surges as lyric, and just as lyricism never wholly disappears from Claudel's dramas, symbolism also remains in the last pieces. The change in dramaturgy is nonetheless recognizable. Where symbolism is dominant in the early dramas, a classical balance in plot structure holds in the dramas with a historical background, and the epic theatre technique is dominant in the last plays. It is significant, however, that though *L'Annonce* was given its definitive form during the last period of Claudel's career, while gaining in objectivity as evidenced by its historical background, its dramaturgy remains what it was from the beginning: it is a play in the best style of symbolism.

The Biblical Theme in *L'Annonce*

The ideas which gave impulse to the creation of *L'Annonce Faite à Marie* were of an intensely personal character. It is a well-known fact that for years, Claudel, the poet-dramatist, had been debating whether to continue a successful career as a diplomat or to leave society in order to dedicate himself solely to God in the religious life. There was, therefore, in him, a powerful attraction to the supernatural with which he formed the character of Violaine in the play. At the same time,

---

[27] Words pronounced after the reading of his poems in the presence of Pope Pius XII. *Ibid.,* p. 237.

he felt strongly drawn to things of the earth, a tendency which he presented in the person of Mara. *L'Annonce Faite à Marie* was the brainchild of an author who had experienced the intense conflict between aspiration to the divine, and fascination to the earthly.

The play revolves around the problem of suffering, like *J. B.* But whereas *J. B.* is an inquiry into the meaning of human pain, *L'Annonce* emphasizes the role of woman as victim through whose suffering the wounds of the world—ecclesial, national and familial—are healed.

On the scene of that Christmas night at Chevoche, we touch the core of Claudel's drama. The feast, which commemorates the union of the divine and the human in Christ at Bethlehem, finds Violaine as the victim offered to God in place of Christianity. The human is exposed to the divine gaze. God accepts the victim and gives His answer symbolized by the return of life to Mara's dead child: the human has once more risen to the sphere of the divine through the immolation of this woman victim whose body is distintegrating due to leprosy.

In this drama, Claudel's conception of woman as victim offered to God is explicit in the words that the dramatist has placed in Violaine's mouth:[28]

> The male is a priest, but it is not forbidden a woman to be the victim. God is avaricious and doesn't allow any creature to be kindled without some impurity being consumed, her own and that round her, like the embers of the censor which are stirred. Today's suffering is everywhere. The people have no father. They look about them and find no king and no pope. That is why my body is suffering in place of

---

[28] Wallace Fowlie's translation, *op. cit.*, p. 100. The original follows:
> Le mâle est prêtre, mais il n'est pas défendu à la femme d'être victime.
> Dieu est avare et ne permet qu'aucume créature soit allumé,
> Sans qu'un peu d'impureté s'y consume.
> La sienne ou celle qui l'entoure, comme la braise de l'encensoir qu'on attise!
> Et certes le malheur de ce temps est grand.
> Ils n'ont point de père. Ils regardent et ne savent plus où est le Roi et le Pape.
> C'est pourquoi voici mon corps en travail à la place de la chrétienté qui se dissout.
> Puissante est la souffrance quand elle est aussi volontaire que le péché!
> **Act III.** *Theatre II,* p. 192.

Christendom as it disintegrates. Suffering is powerful when it is willed as sin is.

It is an interpretation of the Catholic doctrine of the Communion of Saints by which it is believed that the members of the Church which Christ has founded help one another by their prayers, works and sufferings. These, united with Christ, take on a redemptive quality. For the central act in the Church is the Mass which is a continuation of the sacrifice of Christ for men. In every sacrifice, there must be a priest and a victim. Now, the priesthood is reserved to the male, but in Violaine's words, "it is not forbidden a woman to be the victim." In Claudel's vision, it is the role of woman to be the victim suffering for humanity in order to call down God's blessing and pardon.

In *L'Annonce faite à Marie* we are given a glimpse of suffering both in the innocent and in the guilty; various phases of suffering are presented as experienced by the main characters in the play: Violaine, Pierre de Craon, Mara and Jacques.

Pierre de Craon, builder of churches, had been attracted by the beauty of Violaine, and in the heat of passion had attempted to touch the maid, daughter of his own host. Within the year that follows the incident, the mason finds himself afflicted by leprosy which he interprets as his punishment for trying to lay his hands on something sacred. In the prologue of the play, when Violaine bids him good-bye, he explains the gravity of his illness as well as the loneliness of his life. Fully understanding the contagion of his disease, Violaine would nonetheless show him intense compassion, and by so doing aid him to find courage to accomplish the mission that God has entrusted him—that of building His churches away from human relations. This sympathy for the mason, she expresses with the tenderest of gestures: a kiss for this leper, of which Mara is the hidden witness.

Months have passed, and now it is Violaine herself who finds the first traces of the disease appearing on her side. It is at this time, too, that Anne Vercors, her father, whose favorite she is, decides to leave for a pilgrimage to the Holy Land. Before leaving, however, he reveals his intention of ceding his place to Jacques Hury whom he chooses for Violaine's husband. Mara, who is secretly in love with Jacques, and jealous of Violaine, hears this. She then asks their mother to tell Violaine not to marry Jacques; that it is she who must marry him. She herself informs Jacques of the kiss which Violaine had given

Pierre de Craon. Jacques refuses to believe this, however, until he meets Violaine who does not deny Mara's statement. Moreover, he finds that the ring he had given to Violaine is gone, and that Violaine herself had caught Pierre's leprosy. Jacques then thinks of sending her off to the place reserved for lepers at Geyn, while making her mother believe that she is to visit his own mother for some time.

Violaine gone, Mara and Jacques are married and they have a daughter, Aubaine, who is seized with illness and dies. Filled with the passion of a mother, Mara proceeds to look for Violaine at Chevoche. There, in the leper's cave, Mara asks her sister to restore the dead child to life. Despite her reluctance to attempt something she knows she is not worthy to perform, Violaine, out of deep compassion, takes the corpse in her arms and rocks it to and fro, while she asks Mara to read the office [29] for Christmas. At the end of the reading, Mara sees the child moving under Violaine's veil. Her child has come back to life. But when she looks at the child's eyes, she finds that they are now blue as Violaine's while on the child's lips there are drops of milk. And the Angelus sounds at Mon Sanvierge.

The favor received through Violaine has not lessened Mara's jealousy which leads her to push her sister into a trap. Returning from his pilgrimage, Anne Vercors finds his dying daughter unconscious and brings her into his home. He had met Pierre de Craon in the Holy Land, cured of his leprosy. From him, Anne had received the ring which is now back on Violaine's finger. Then Anne explains Violaine's sacrifice: like Mary she had conceived of the Holy Spirit— conceived the great sorrow of the world around her, of the Church split in the great schism, and that of France for whom Jeanne is to give her life. All this Violaine had seen,[30] and it was with the intention of offering herself to call down God's mercy that she had kissed the leper, fully knowing what she was doing.

Toward the end, Violaine is brought back temporarily to consciousness by the song of a child outdoors. Her last words, "How good it is to live! and how immense is God's glory. . . . But it is also good to die when it is well ended and little by little the obscurity spreads

---

[29] Office: The prayers of the Church designated for recitation daily, varying for each feast celebrated for the day.

[30] Cf. words of Anne Vercors in the last act.

over us like a very dim shadow,"[31] are followed by the ringing of the
Angelus bells with their message of

> Peace, Peace, Peace
> Glory to God in the highest and on earth peace
>   to men of good will
>   Rejoice
>   Rejoice
>   Rejoice [32]

while Anne Vercors takes Mara's hand and Jacques' which he raises
solemnly in a gesture of oblation. Jacques and Mara look fixedly at
each other while the bells continue ringing.

Such is the story. In *L'Annonce,* Claudel has drawn the meaning
of suffering in no uncertain lines. First and foremost, he gives a redemptive meaning to suffering. In the same way that Christ accepted
suffering for the salvation of the human race, Violaine accepts the
suffering of leprosy and gives up her lover in order to satisfy her sister;
she takes on herself the bodily curse that was Pierre de Craon's;
she lives abandoned; she is jeered at, considered the refuse of men,
so that the Church of Christ may be healed of the great schism.
However, in the sacrifice of Christ, He was both priest and victim;
Violaine sees herself as the woman who is "not forbidden to be the
victim."

Now, Violaine's acceptance of the role of suffering has its prototype in Mary's *Fiat.* Hence, the title, *L'Annonce faite à Marie.* The
tidings brought to Mary were that she would become mother of the
Savior. While remaining a virgin, Mary would give birth to Christ
through the working of the Holy Spirit. The suffering of her Son

---

[31] Paul Claudel, *Theatre II,* p. 214. In the original:
> Que c'est beau de vivre! et que la gloire de Dieu
est immense!
> Mais que c'est bon aussi
> De mourir alors que c'est bien fini et que s'étend
sur nous peu à peu
> L'obscurcissement comme d'un ombrage très obscur.
[32] In the original:
> Pax pax pax
> Pax pax pax
> Père père père
Gloria in excelsis Deo et in terra pax hominibus bonae voluntatis
> Laetare
> Lae ta re
> Lae ta re!

would also be Mary's own; she would stand at the foot of the Cross to witness His agony. Violaine's answer to the demand of Providence made of her was the same as Mary's: "Behold the handmaid of the Lord." She was to be the virgin through whose oblation the broken Church would be given rebirth. By her intense prayer and generous forgiveness, she would become mother to Mara's child reborn into life through the agony of a leper.

As has been previously mentioned, the drama embodies the Catholic doctrine of the Communion of Saints which is a favorite theme of Claudel's. It is a theme drawn from Christ's words: "I am the vine: you the branches. He that abideth in me and I in him, the same beareth much fruit: for without me you can do nothing." (John, xv:5). In the words of St. Paul, "...we, though many, are one body in Christ, and individually members of one another." (Romans, xii: 5). Every member of the Church is so united with Christ that His suffering takes on the redemptive value of Christ's Passion. Moreover, whatever one member does affects the whole mystical body. Thus, Claudel assumes that with the offering of Violaine as victim, the problems of the Vercors, of France and of Christendom were solved.

Yet, Claudel also recognizes the purifying value of suffering. To Pierre de Craon, leprosy was a punishment and a means of atonement for sin. So was the anguish of jealousy and misunderstanding between Mara and Jacques the agony that follows guilt. Toward the end of the play, the gesture of oblation by means of which Mara and Jacques, as man and wife, accepted the anguish that would remain in their wedded life, reminds us of the acceptance of suffering by the first man and woman whose guilt condemned them to a life of pain. It is not the same kind of saintly acceptance that Violaine made, for hers was the generous offering of herself as Christ had done in undeserved pain. Mara's and Jacques' affirmation was that of the ordinary human beings who plod on in the effort to give God what is His due, so that pain is accepted, if not with full volition, at least with resignation.

Growth of a Mystery Play: The Dramatist's Vision

Considering the metamorphosis of Claudel's play from the first version of *La Jeune Fille Violaine* in 1892 to the final version of

L'Annonce faite à Marie in 1948, we find ourselves engaged in a fascinating study of how the development of an idea left its traces on dramaturgy.

It was on the evening of Christmas in 1886, after the memorable vespers at Notre Dame, that Claudel returned home and opened his sister Camille's Bible. His eyes lighted on the Gospel narrative of the incident at Emmaus and on chapter eight of the *Book of Proverbs* which revealed to him the symbolism of woman. Thenceforth, Claudel could think of woman only in the light of this symbolism: she is wisdom, or grace, she is the Virgin, she is the Church, she is the human soul.[33]

The first woman in Claudel's dramas revealing the influence of the *Book of Proverbs* is the Princess in *Tête d'Or*. This drama, however, centers around the hero, Simon Agnel. It is in *L'Annonce faite à Marie* that Claudel embodies the fullness of his idea of woman. But it took him fifty-six years to make this idea come out in the play which is considered his favorite work as a dramatist. And as the idea developed into a vision, the drama took shape.

In the first version of *La Jeune Fille Violaine*, the idea brought out is that of woman as wisdom or grace. Joy is the keynote of the first act where Violaine is seen against the background of washing day in the country. There is the bustle of children coming in and out in a holiday mood, asking their *maraine* to tell them a story. And Violaine moves about as a daughter of light, loved by all and doing good to everybody, even to her sister Bibiane who is the only antagonist in the play. There is gaiety of movement which is carried on to the third act where the heroine is shown as the holy woman whose aid is being sought by a countless number of people. All through, Violaine is grace; through her suffering she brings blessings to others, gives sight to Bibiane's child, conciliates Baube and Lidine who have been married without mutual love, and teaches Jacquin Uri and Bibiane the patient endurance of the difficulties of life. Violaine is also wisdom revealing what she has learned from experience, that suffering is not evil.[34] The rainbow that spans the sky in the last act is meant to convey the idea of peace which comes to a soul that has lived a life of holiness, the peace that she also brings to those around her.

---

[33] Louis Chaigne, *op. cit.*, pp. 50-51.
[34] Il n'est pas mauvais de souffrir! il n'est pas mauvais de souffrir. (*Théâtre I*, p. 550).

By 1898, Claudel's idea of Violaine has developed from that of the child of grace and joy to that of the virgin—the human soul that represents our highest aspirations. To portray this, the dramatist has effected certain distinctive changes of dramaturgy. Instead of the noise and bustle of the scene of country washing at the opening of the play, there is the silence of dawn during the conversation between Pierre de Craon, builder of churches, and Violaine who has understood his meaning. And the kiss she gives him is the expression of the consecration of their lives to the will of God. At the end of the play, it is Pierre de Craon who finds Violaine dying and brings her into the house of the Vercors. He comes back in time to see the end of that life which, together with his, has been consecrated. And he offers thanksgiving for holiness in her life, stirring himself to live, as she had done, in intimate communion with God, like the vine and the olive tree.[35] Only six years separate the writing of the first version from that of the second, but between the two versions there is a vast difference attesting to a deepening of the poet's spirit during the intervening years. For in the second version, the very beginning is on a supernatural level reached by the first version only much later in the play.

It will be noticed, moreover, that in the second version, the dramatist, in changing the name of Violaine's sister from Bibiane to Mara, has made a significant alteration. The name Violaine, with its affinity to the words of violin and violet, is a compound of sweetness in music, in fragrance and in appearance. It is suggestive of the finer aspirations of the human soul, of that which is heavenly in man. The name Mara, which means "bitter," is suggestive of the things of the earth, of the passions that war against the soul. From the structure of the miracle play in the first version of *La Jeune Fille Violaine,* Claudel evolved a kind of morality play with the strengthening of the idea of conflict between the forces of good and of evil in the person of Violaine and Mara.

When Claudel changed the title of his play into *L'Annonce faite à Marie* in 1911, the evolution from miracle to mystery play had reached its completion. With the ringing of the Angelus, Violaine

---

[35] Que je vive ainsi! que je grandisse ainsi, melange à mon Dieu, comme la vigne et l'olivier! (*Ibid.,* p. 656).

repeats the words of the Virgin Mary: "Behold the handmaid of the Lord; be it done to me according to Thy word." And with Mary she accepts the mission that God is giving her in life: the mission of suffering, as was Christ's, for the salvation of the world. Like Mary, Violaine was to be another Christ; as Christ was wounded from the crown of His head to the sole of His feet, Violaine would bear the wounds of leprosy. She would be a living soul in a dying body. And at her death, in the words of Anne Vercors, "The earth is liberated," the family of the Vercors is freed from the sorrow of death, for little Aubaine has come back to life; Jacques and Mara have been freed from a marriage based on falsehood, and now they are ready to begin life anew; France is free from sorrow, for now her king has been crowned; and the Church is cured of the tearing wound of schism, for now a true Pope has been given her.

Claudel further develops the idea of Violaine as another Mary when he makes the miracle of Aubaine's coming back to life at Christmas. Pressed to the bosom of Violaine the leper, Aubaine regains life just when the church bells are ringing the "Gloria in Excelsis Deo!" (Glory to God in the Highest!). And Violaine continues, "Peace on earth...a child is born to us." Through the prayer and suffering of a virgin, a child is reborn. Once more, like Mary, a virgin has brought forth a child to the world.

The final version written in 1948 gives us no essential change in the idea brought out by the 1911 version. Changes in dramaturgy show only an effort to make the idea still clearer. Pierre de Craon does not come back in the fourth act, thus disappearing after fulfilling his mystical role of making Violaine's mission clear. Through Anne Vercors, whom he meets in Jerusalem, he sends back the ring that Violaine has given him. Thus, in this final version, this sign of Violaine's acceptance of her vocation is to be back on her finger at death as a sign of her claim to eternal life after the life of suffering during which her promise to God has been fulfilled. The shortening of Anne Vercors' speeches at the end of the play serves to focus the attention of the audience on the essential point, which is that of Violaine's consecration demanding also the consecration in the lives of those around her. This is clinched by the gesture with which Claudel makes the definitive version end: In front of the dead Violaine, the victim offered to God, Jacques and Mara join hands which Anne Vercors raises as a symbol of their own oblation united with the victim.

The doing away of the chorus of angels in Latin in the third act may be interpreted as an attempt to adapt dramaturgy to the taste of the audience. Similarly, instead of making Violaine and Pierre de Craon recite the Angelus aloud in the Prologue, Claudel leaves them to pray in silence, so that only the ringing of the bells can be heard reverberating over the scene. This may also be regarded as expressive of the interior silence of the soul in harmony with the sublimity of the mystery.

To Claudel, the idea of woman which struck him on that memorable Christmas Day at Notre Dame grew into the proportions of a vision of woman's role on the plane of the supernatural. To present this vision dramatically, Claudel needed to appeal to the whole man, not only as a being capable of reasoning, but as one with the capacity to envision by intuition happenings that are beyond the senses, the power to enter into a presentation of life that surpasses the natural.

The Symbolism in *L'Annonce faite a Marie*

Contrasted with the realistic approach of the epic theatre employed by MacLeish, Claudel's symbolism in *L'Annonce faite à Marie* is of the same spirit as Coleridge's who claimed that "The poet, described in ideal perfection brings the whole soul of man into activity, with the subordination of its faculties to each other, according to their relative worth and dignity."[36] Whereas MacLeish devoted a great part of his play to the attempt to make a rational presentation of suffering man, Claudel starts with the assumption that suffering can be so sublimated as to be pleasing to God and draw down His blessing not only on the sufferer but also on those for whom this sufferer is the holocaust. Claudel demands not a mere intellectual response but a ready exercise of the imagination, and a willingness to acquiesce in the harmonious movement of the emotions. The success of the performance of a play based on an assumption like Claudel's will depend on the audience's ability to appreciate and share in the dramatist's vision.

By the background he chooses, Claudel brings his audience back to the Middle Ages where the atmosphere of faith is genuine. There is no room in this background for the skepticism of the twentieth

---

[36] S.T. Coleridge, *Biographia Literaria, Vol. II,* ed. J. Shawcross (London: Oxford University Press, 1962), p. 12.

century. Claudel addresses his play not to the skeptics but to the pure of heart—the believers in "the Kingdom." From the very start he takes the faith of the audience for granted and proposes a joint adventure with them into a realm where faith has the purity of sainthood.

If MacLeish's method is intellectual, Claudel's is intuitive. He accomplishes his aim not through argument but through the subtlety of suggestion through the analogue which is identical with what Auerbach terms *figura,* and T.S. Eliot, the "mythical method."[37] According to Auerbach, "Figural prophecy implies the interpretation of one worldly event through another...the first signifies the second and the second fulfills the first. Both remain historical events, yet both, looked at in this way, have something provisional and incomplete about them; they point to each other and both point to something in the future...which will be the actual, real, and definitive event."[38] In *L'Annonce*, Violaine's acceptance of her mission of suffering points to that of Mary whose consent to her role in the redemption of humanity was a prototype to all such cooperation in Christ's mission. Moreover, Mary's and Violaine's acceptance of God's will points to the state of perfect union of the creature's will to the Creator's which will be accomplished in eternity.

In Claudel's drama, at the crucial moment when life is about to return to the dead child, the very gestures that Claudel makes Violaine perform call back to our mind an image of the Virgin Mother on that night of the first Christmas; she bids Mara "Read it to God. Read it to the angels. Read it to all the earth." And she adds: "As for me, I shall enter into the night beneath my night to listen to you." Then she goes down to the interior of the ruins which shelter her, and remains there with the child beneath the veil falling over her bosom as Mara reads. During that first Christmas, the Virgin brought forth a child to redeem a sinful world. This Christmas in the ruins, the prayer of a virgin suffering the living death of leprosy makes God breathe life back into the Vercors, the child of the woman who had been responsible for Violaine's being forsaken in a state of misery.

The motherhood of Mary and the motherhood of Violaine in turn, prefigure that state of the blessed whose glory will consist in the

---

37 Cf. p. 37 of this book.
38 Erich Auerbach, "Figura," *Scenes from the Drama of European Literature: Six Essays* (New York: Meridian), pp. 59-60.
See also *Mimesis* (Garden City, New York; 1957), pp. 64-66, 136-41, 170-76.

perfection of their abiding by God's will in eternity. For, as Christ said, "Whosoever shall do the will of my Father that is in heaven, he is my brother, and sister and mother." (Matt. xii, 50).

In order to make the analogy of Violaine and the Virgin clear, the dramatist makes use of various devices suggesting the inner life of the characters or even the inner meaning of the events.

Pervading the whole play is the ringing of the Angelus heard in varying tones. Now, to the Christian world, the sound of Angelus bells is immediately associated with the Virgin Mary's "Fiat!"—her acceptance of the will of God as announced to her by the angel. It is also a constant reminder of the mystery of Christmas in "the Word... made flesh" to redeem the world. The first time the ringing of the bells can be heard in the play is at the prologue. It is almost morning, and the Violaine who comes to bid good-bye to Pierre de Craon, to tell him that he has been pardoned, is also in the morning of her life. She is a happy being who loves and is loved: she is, in her own words, a being made for joy. And the bells that ring during this scene are those of Easter with their message of rejoicing: "Regina Coeli, laetare, alleluia!" (Rejoice, Queen of Heaven! Alleluia!) It is during this season of gladness that Violaine understands the role of pain given her by God. And she accepts it.

In the second act we are in the middle of the year. It is noon, and the nuns of Monsanvierge (the convent supported by the Vercors family) intone the *Salve Regina*, a prayer pleading to Mary to remember those who are struggling in this "valley of tears." Violaine discovers the signs of the fatal disease on her. The secret of her leprosy which she is about to reveal will change her relations with her fiancé, with her family and with the world. The mission which Violaine had accepted in the Prologue has become actuality, the grimness of which makes even this brave girl put out her hand at the end of this act in a very human gesture seeking for something to support her.

When the bells sound the third time, it is the midnight of Christmas. As the *Gloria* of the Midnight Mass is heard, Violaine asks Mara to read the Office of Christmas. And as the reading ends, the dead child on Violaine's bosom begins to show signs of life. Violaine's words re-echo lines from the Gospel of Christmas: "To us too, a child is born. I give you tidings of great joy....Glory be to God! Peace to men on earth." And the bells of Monsanvierge sound in the distance.

On the night of the anniversary of Christ's birth, an heir is assured to the Vercors.

The last time the bells will be heard ringing is at dawn, at the end of the last scene, as though to announce the entrance into glory of one whose life had been one long "Fiat!"

Together with the symbolism conveyed through the various tones of the Angelus bells, we should consider the subtle association aroused by the songs of children and of birds. Most impressive of these is the child's verset recited toward the end of the play:

> Marguerite de Paris
> Prete-moi tes souliers gris
> Pour aller en paradis!
> Qu'il fait beau!
> Qu'il fait chaud!
> J'entends le petit oiseau
> Qui fait pi i i i![39]

The child's voice reaches Violaine's subconsciousness. Silent up to this time in what seemed to be the unconsciousness preceding death, Violaine recognizes the song which she had, as a child, sung with Mara. And she remembers the joy and the innocence of childhood. Thus, the song, associated with innocence, suggests the state of soul which Violaine has retained up to the moment of her death. A more remote symbolism of the child's song is the suggestion of the eternal innocence of God which had struck Claudel that Christmas of 1886. For the spirit of Violaine's resembles God's, owing to the union of their wills accomplished by the active "Fiat" which took her a lifetime to utter in its fullness.

Earlier in the play, the cuckoo's song—Mi di! Mi di! la-bas! la-bas!—occurring at the moment when Anne Vercors bids good-bye to his household at Combernon, is an echo of the feeling of his family. It is more effective than if any personage had expressed his thoughts,

---

[39] Marguerite of Paris
Lend me your gray slippers
To go to Paradise!
How beautiful the world!
How warm it is.
I hear the bird
Go pip! pip! pip!
(Wallace Fowlie, *ibid.,* p. 131)

speaking of the uncertainty felt because of the distance that Anne is to travel in going to the Holy Land.

Another important symbol used in the play is the ring which Violaine gives to Pierre de Craon to aid him to build the church of the child martyr, Justitia. Violaine's act of giving the ring, which she has received from her fiancé, is suggestive of her offering to God that for which the ring stands: a happy family life with the man who loved her and whom she herself loved.

Of subordinate significance in the symbolism of the play are certain metaphors employed by the dramatist. Though not one of these has the same unifying effect as the symbolism of the Angelus, they nonetheless enrich the play with the beauty of their suggestiveness. Thus in the Prologue, Pierre de Craon speaks of Violaine as the lark praising God in the joyousness of her life: "Sing at high heaven, lark of France!"[40] At the moment when a cloud of sadness comes over Pierre at the thought of the lonely life he is to lead on the steeples of churches, Violaine recalls to him the symbol of the paschal candle which is consumed little by little for the glory of the whole Church.[41] While devoting himself to the building of churches, Pierre, devoured by leprosy, is compared to the candle which burns itself in the service of God. In the last act, the time is that of harvest. The season chosen by Claudel for the end of the play is symbolical of the fecundity of Violaine's life of suffering and prayer. At her death she has obtained all that she had prayed for: for her family, for her country and for the whole Church.

In its use of the analogue, oblique suggestion and metaphor, Claudel's symbolism follows traditional methods of figurative expression. But in the use of silences, it aligns itself with the symbolism of Maeterlinck. The "Claudelian beyond" is a world of faith in which the natural comes in touch with the supernatural. Like the "Maeterlinckian beyond,"[42] it is a world of feeling, but feeling that elicits depths of

---

40 Fowlie, *ibid.,* p. 17. In the original: Chante au plus haut du ciel alouette de France! (*Theâtre II,* p. 142).

41 Soyez un homme, Pierre! Soyez digne de la flamme qui vous consume!
    Et s'il faut être dévoré que ce soit sur un candélabre
        d'or comme la Cierge Pascal en plein choeur pour
        la gloire de toute l'Église! (*Theâtre II,* p. 143).

42 A term which the French dramatic critic Francisque Sarcey (1827-99) had used in contempt, the "Maeterlinckian beyond" aptly describes "the invisible place which is just beyond the place of action." cf. Donald Clive Stuart,

thought. It is feeling whose explanation is better left to be intuitively followed by the reader.

On reading *L'Annonce* one is struck by the fact that among the directions contained in the play, the instruction for "silence" outnumbers all the others. True to the ways of symbolism as practiced by dramatists like Maeterlinck, when words cannot convey the fullness of meaning desired, Claudel has recourse to silence—a silence that pushes the meaning to a "beyond" which has even greater reality than that perceived directly by the senses. Silences occur during moments of intense feeling, of weighty realizations, overpowering recognitions.

Among the multitude of silences with which the play is fraught, I shall try to pick out a few. There is the silence of one who is incapable of putting her impression of some personage into words, as when Mara tells her mother of her intention to kill herself if Violaine marries Jacques (Act I, Scene 2). The mother can find no words with which to express what she feels. And her exclamation, "O tête!" followed by silence, is more remarkable for what it leaves unsaid than for what it does say. This silence, of course, is more eloquent than if she had said, "What a pigheaded girl you are! When you have ideas, there is no knowing where they will lead you," etc. Had the mother said all this, the effect would have been dissipated, whereas the weight is concentrated on the two words, "O tête!"

There is the silence of doubt. In Scene Three of the same act, the mother asks: "How long a time will you stay there?" And Anne Vercors answers: "I don't know. Perhaps a very short time. I shall be back soon."[43] The silence that follows allows space for the reflections of those who listen to his words. For the majority among them are filled with a sense of uncertainty. It is possible that he may never come back.

There are moments of sorrow, as well as those characterized by a mixture of emotions passing within: in Violaine's case, there is filial love for and submission to her father, love for her fiancé, the confrontation with the facts of life and of alterations in her condition

---

The Development of Dramatic Art (New York: Dover Publications, 1960), pp. 628-35.

    43 Fowlie, *ibid.*, p. 46. The original:
      La Mère: Combien de temps vas-tu rester là-bas?
      Anne Vercors: Je ne sais. Peu de temps peut-être.
        Bientôt je suis de retour.
              (*Théâtre II*, p. 160)

which produce an overwhelming sense of awe and sudden strangeness all beyond her power to formulate into words. Thus in the second act, when Mara informs her of their mother's death, silence ensues. Too many thoughts crowd into her mind to find an outlet, thoughts on the cause of her death, and of all that has happened since then; thoughts of the past scenes with her mother, of their adieu when the facts had to remain unsaid. The silence is fraught with a sense of all these.

Then too, there is the silence that accompanies dramatic irony. As Violaine announces her intention to leave the house, her mother opens her arms to embrace her daughter. But Violaine says that she has made a vow not to let anyone touch her. And Mara, although sensing that Violaine is to leave them for good, asks: "Until your return?" And there is silence. Of the four persons present in the scene—Jacques, Mara, Violaine and the mother—it is only the last one who has not yet divined the answer to the question; she alone is ignorant of Violaine's disease, although she may have felt presentiments that Violaine would no longer return.

Claudel can also express the silence of those grown wise by experience. In the opening scene of the last act, Mara and Jacques are pretending that Anne Vercors has come back; their dialogue is a burlesque of the imagined scene of his return; doing a mock curtsy, Mara, greeting an imagined guest, says:

> Not here at the moment, my Lord! When people go off to Jerusalem, they shouldn't expect to find everything the same. Seven years is a long time. Now it's Mara who occupies her place at the corner of the fire.[44]

Anne Vercors has appeared during the scene, apparently divining the course of the dialogue. But he makes no comment on the make-believe. His simple, "Bonjour, Jacques! Bonjour, Mara!" is saturated with understanding and wisdom and pardon. The silence that follows on the part of Mara and Jacques, caught in their burlesque, is one of shame and awe.

---

44 Fowlie, *ibid.,* p. 120. In the original:
   Pas ici pour le moment, Monseigneur! Dame, quand
      on va à Jerusalem faut pas s'attendre à retrouver
      tout le monde! C'est long, sept ans!
   C'est Mara maintenant qui occupe sa place au coin
      du feu.
                    (*Théâtre II,* p. 203)

The deepest silences, however, are those before the most weighty realities of life. Such was Jacques' silence when Violaine showed him the first trace of leprosy appearing on her flank. Such was the silence at the close of the play—the silence of Violaine accepting death, too; the silence of Jacques and Mara realizing the pains that they are to live over again, after the disguises have been torn away; and the silence of Anne Vercors foreseeing the difficulty, but sublimating it into an oblation. And these silences make up a great silence overflowing with the reverberation of Easter bells with their promise of peace and joy.

In the study of the dramaturgy of *L'Annonce,* we have noticed the role of symbolism. Although the playwriting of Claudel progressed from symbolism to epic theatre, it is significant that in writing this drama with a biblical theme, he adheres to the ways of symbolism.[45]

The epic theatre dramaturgy of MacLeish aims at a *verfremdung,* an alienation of the audience so that, on the whole, what is demanded of them is a critical process. On the other hand, the symbolism employed by Claudel in *L'Annonce* effects an emotional identification of the audience with the characters of the play in accordance with the Aristotelian theory of katharsis. In contemplating Violaine, the spectators are moved to pity for the extreme pain, physical and moral, which she undergoes. Yet, this feeling of pity is steeped with admiration for the nobility of this Claudelian heroine. On the other hand, Jacques' and Mara's plight, precipitated through their own fault, arouses in us, over and above pity, the feeling of fear upon the recognition of the justice with which they are being chastised with the very weapon they have unjustly used. For love's sake, Mara has betrayed her sister. And now, this love of Jacques which she has temporarily succeeded in gaining, at least outwardly, gives way to contempt upon his discovery of the falsehood on which it has been founded.

In presenting conflicting emotions in *L'Annonce,* Claudel is the master striving for and achieving the harmony of emotion and thought to bring out the meaning of suffering in human life. To arrive at that

---

45 Two other biblical pieces written by Claudel about this time—*L'Histoire de Tobie et de Sara* and *Le Festin de la Sagesse*—are epic theatre in style, but these differ from *L'Annonce* in that they are biblical commentaries rather than presentations of life.

unity, to form that impression of meaning in the providential design found in life, to accomplish the beauty of design, Claudel has employed a dramaturgy which is a synthesis of symbolism traditional and modern.

CHAPTER FOUR

The Language Employed
for Biblical Themes

Giving too much consideration to the dramaturgy of a play can give the impression that dramaturgy is everything. There is nothing so misleading, however, as to suggest that once a dramatist supplied with a theme has decided on his dramaturgy, the play writes itself quite naturally. The choice of dramaturgy implies the selection of the language with which to clothe it, and the writing of the play will mean a constant grappling with the problem of language. For it is through the language of the play that the author's technique comes home to us. It is, therefore, impossible to think of dramaturgy without at the same time considering the language employed in it. It is possible even to conceive of a play in which the success of the technique rests wholly on the language employed.

Since, roughly speaking, half of the dramas being studied in this book are written in prose, and the other half in verse, the simplest procedure in studying the language they use would seem to be to classify these dramas into prose dramas and verse dramas. The division into prose and verse is nevertheless unsatisfactory. Although verse has generally been the vehicle of poetry, verse dramas are not necessarily all-poetic; on the other hand, some parts of the prose pieces rise to the level of poetry. Rather than follow the arbitrary classification into prose and verse, I shall consider how the aim of the dramatist has determined the language he uses in the play. And the language employed likewise reveals the spirit in which the biblical theme is being handled.

THE DIALECTIC OF IMMEDIACY

Dramatists of our time are confronted by two requisites for success. According to T.S. Eliot, the writer of our century should be difficult, for "Our civilization comprehends great variety and complexity, and this variety and complexity, playing upon a refined sensibility, must produce various and complex results. The poet must become more and more comprehensive, more allusive, more indirect, in order to force, to dislocate if necessary, language into its meaning."[1] Yet, the dramatist who is also a poet in his own right, while complying with the demand of difficulty, cannot afford to remain in an ivory tower. More than any other writer, the dramatist needs to court his audience. The struggle to weld difficulty with popularity has led some of our dramatists to handle biblical themes in the spirit of argumentation. In this, the dramatist's proximate aim is to throw out a challenge to his audience, to draw it away from its intellectual sloth and complacency, to involve it in a dramatized discussion or debate. To accomplish his purpose, the dramatist must have vigorous language at his command—the language that can hold the attention of an audience by its immediate appeal. While integrating biblical themes which are drawn from the past, the dramatist must use the language of the present.

J.B.: Discussion in Verse

To dissipate suspicions of esotericism, MacLeish writes his dialogues in terms the modern mind can understand. First of all, he presents the problem of suffering in the concrete: through disease and the losses that come from the atom bomb and its kind. With these palpable instances to build on, he develops his dialectic on human suffering. And before it is aware of what is happening, the audience is being drawn into taking sides in a discussion of the meaning of human suffering. The conclusion to which it is led is that suffering is meaningless, and yet men and women can accept it not for the love of God, but because they love one another. To arrive at this conclusion,

---

[1] *T.S. Eliot*, "The Metaphysical Poets," *Selected Essays* (London: Faber and Faber, 1963), p. 289.

MacLeish becomes a kind of iconoclast, blasting the image of a sentimentally good and loving God.

Now, invective lends itself to the uses of iconoclasm, and Mac-Leish is at his best in the epithet of abuse.[2] It is interesting to analyze the means by which the dramatist achieves vigor of language in *J. B.*

There is sufficient elasticity in the verse of *J. B.* to portray various moods. MacLeish's tetrameter lines, now and then relieved by penta-meter verses, can be made to depict the conversation of pleasant everyday life in a family, as well as heated arguments between the God-mask and the Satan-mask, the cynicism of comforters as well as the flashes of loveliness at the close of the play. This is a sign of the ability to so appropriate an old rhythm as to make it flexible to the needs of stagecraft.

MacLeish's iambic tetrameters, moreover, are often accented by an alliteration which gives verve and pungency to the language, as when Nickles says:

> Look at those *l*ips: they've tasted something
> *B*itter as a *b*roth of *b*lood.
> And *s*pat the *s*up out. (p. 19)

Here and there the alliteration becomes onomatopoeia:

> Job wishes!—
> Thinks there should be justice somewhere—
> *B*eats his *b*ones against the glass. (p. 17)

> Pounding his *b*eat by the *b*ack of the lumberyard
> Somebody runs and he yells and they stumble—
> Big kid—nineteen maybe—
> Hopped to the eyes and scared—scared
> *B*loodless he could *b*arely *b*reathe.
> Constable yanks him up *b*y the *b*ritches. (p. 82)

MacLeish's alliteration has the knack of suggesting feeling. Notice the irony in the lines:

> Never fails! Never fails!
> Count on you to make a mess of it!
> Every *b*lessed *b*lundering time
> You hit at one man you blast thousands. (p. 99)

---

[2] This is noticeable in his plays: *Nobodaddy, Panic, The Trojan Horse* and *The Fall of the City.*

The intensity of horror can be felt in the following:

> God has shut the night against me.
> God has set the dark alight
> With horror *b*lazing *b*lind as day
> When I go toward it . . . (p. 108)

Epithets are made unforgettable because they are alliterated: "stale *p*ink *p*ill" (p. 95), "*c*old *c*omforters" (p. 112), "*p*utrid *p*oultice of the soul" (p. 112).

As MacLeish eliminated the rhyme when using terza rima in *Conquistador,* so in *J. B.* he has employed an unrhymed iambic tetrameter to suit his purposes. When he introduces rhyme, however, it is in view of a certain effect. Now and then, in the midst of highly rhetorical lines, he suddenly inserts a sort of singsong that has the effect of parody:

> Those stars that stare their stares at me—
> Are those the staring stars I see
> Or only lights. . .
>   not meant for me? (p. 5)

The above-quoted lines remind us of others from Macbeth's soliloquy, though they are but a stale echo of the Shakespearean lines. When the singsong is not a parody, it may take the form of evident ridicule, thus:

> Nevertheless the mask is imperative.
> If God should laugh
> The mare would calf
> The cow would foal:
> Diddle my soul. . . (p. 8)

As those of T.S. Eliot in his most serious poems, the nursery rhymes in *J. B.* have the effect of stirring the consciousness to some half-forgotten melody. In the final lines of Scene One, for all their almost childish simplicity, there lurks a feeling of foreboding which is a key to the tragedy:

> I love Monday, Tuesday, Wednesday.
> Where have Monday, Tuesday, gone?
> Under the grass tree,
> Under the green tree,
> One by one.

> Caught as we are in Heaven's quandary,
> Is it they or we are gone
> Under the grass tree
> Under the green tree? (p. 43)

In the language of the play, MacLeish brings out a great contrast between the biblical quotations spoken by the God-mask and the Satan-mask as well as by The Voice, and the ordinary though highly accented language of the characters involved in the plot. The impression given is that of a gap between the invisible and the visible. The enormous difference between the biblical language employed and the everyday speech of the characters presents the natural as highly contrasted with the supernatural. It is as if the faith of the New England banker and his family were a thing of the past, with but flimsy vestiges in the present. The biblical quotations have been inserted to cast an atmosphere of solemnity by their evoking associations in the memories of the audience. Moreover, they serve to make a framework for the play by establishing a parallelism with the Bible narrative.

The images MacLeish creates produce powerful effects. They make an impact that shakes one out of complacency, arousing the tendency to evaluate figures of speech for what they are worth, instead of lulling one into the pleasing sensations of the sweetly beautiful. Notice the unexpected adjective associated with a star in the following lines:

> Horrible as a star above
> A burning, murdered, broken city. . . (p. 20)

The Sartrean attitude can be felt in the blasphemous epithet:

> Job will make his own cold peace
> When God pursues him in the web too far—
> Implacable, eternal Spider. (pp. 94-95)

By far the most convincing lines in the play are spoken by Nickles whose role is more that of commentator than of actor. His speech, representing modern cynicism and sardonic sarcasm, possesses a relevance which gives his voice the quality of actuality. Its truth is that of psychology and of fact. His lines possess the vigor of the invective.

J. B. is verse drama in which two voices predominate: the voice of the sneering cynic in Nickles (Satan-mask), and the voice of

MacLeish himself making itself heard in the best lines of Sarah and of J. B. By means of these voices, possessed of both strength and sensitivity, the appeal is made to a heterogeneous audience: to the believing as well as to the unbelieving, to the intellectual as well as to the sentimental.

To reach his heterogeneous audience, MacLeish somehow had to make a compromise. Hence, despite the indisputable presence of poetry in his verses, despite his masterly handling of poetical devices, MacLeish's continual preoccupation with argument prevents his language from rising to poetic grandeur. It is language adapted to the multitude that attends the theater: retaining the beauty of verse for the more sensitive, but often reminiscent of a highly eloquent, combative prose, for those of a more argumentative turn of mind.

Back to Methuselah: Discussion in Prose

Half a century ahead of MacLeish, Shaw had expounded discussion as a technical novelty for post-Ibsen plays.[3] However, realizing the disadvantages of placing the discussion at the end of a play as Ibsen had done, when the audience was fatigued, Shaw contrived to present the discussion first, or even to make it interpenetrate the action. In this point, MacLeish was Shavian rather than Ibsenian in his use of discussion.

However, where MacLeish essayed the return to verse for argumentation in *J. B.*, Shaw employed the expository medium of prose in *Back to Methuselah*. In developing his theory of creative evolution as "the path to the godhead," through men's use of their "tremendous miracle-working force of will" to lengthen their life span in the "pursuit of omnipotence and omniscience," the dramatist dedicates the first scene to a general discussion of such subjects as death, love and birth. This discussion then serves as a foundation for the discovery made in the second scene, that death was the "invention" of the first man who could not bear the thought of living on forever. This discovery becomes a conviction—a gospel—explained by the Barnabas Brothers in Part II. Their program "is only that the term of human

---

[3] "The Quintessence of Ibsenism," *Major Critical Essays*. First published in 1891; reprinted, London: Constable and Co., 1955.

life shall be extended to three hundred years." They claim: "We can put it into men's heads that there is nothing to prevent its happening but their own will to die before their work is done, and their own ignorance of the splendid work there is for them to do.... Spread that knowledge and that conviction; and as surely as the sun will rise tomorrow, the thing will happen."

Of Ibsen, Shaw had written that "He gives us not only ourselves, but ourselves in our own situations. The things that happen to his stage figures are things that happen to us."[4] Now, in the First Act of *Back to Methuselah,* this is exactly what Shaw does: he gives us ourselves in our situations, and, we may add, in our own language. Nothing could be more remote from our everyday life than the theory of creative evolution and the story of Adam and Eve. Yet, in the language of Shaw, we find ourselves following the discussions held by Adam, Eve and The Serpent. "Rhetoric, irony, argument, paradox, epigram, parable and the rearrangement of haphazard facts into orderly and intelligent situations: these are both the oldest and newest arts of the drama," Shaw had claimed.[5] The enrichment of the First Act with these very "arts" makes it refreshing material to both audience and reader.

At the opening dialogue between Adam and Eve, there is a naiveté that would be expected in a pair to whom the world was new. Their speech moves in staccatos as they come across death in an animal for the first time. But as they consider the meaning of death in its applicability to themselves, their utterance begins to lengthen into balanced and periodic sentences, a contrast which is very effective in expressing inexperience and the advent of maturity with its endless complexities.

Shaw sprinkles this first act with the epigram, the paradox and the rhetorical question that spring spontaneously and belong where they sprout. "Death is not an unhappy thing when you have learnt how to conquer it," says The Serpent. Elsewhere it declares, "Love may be too long a word for so short a thing soon. But when it is short, it will be very sweet." There is wit in The Serpent who finds the right comment for everything: "The woman knows that there is no such thing as nothing: the man knows that there is no such day as tomor-

4 *Ibid.*
5 *Ibid.*

row." Because of its uncanny role of tempter, The Serpent speaks in accents of pseudo-wisdom, hence the tendency to utter epigrams. The paradox, too, comes to it very naturally: "...nothing is certain but uncertainty."

We follow the first man and woman through their process of learning the names for ideas, and the experience becomes an engrossing adventure. When The Serpent declares that once death is conquered it is no longer an unhappy thing, the following conversation takes place:

> *Eve.* How can I conquer it?
> *The Serpent.* By another thing, called birth.
> *Eve.* What? (Trying to pronounce it) B-birth?
> *The Serpent.* Yes, birth.
> *Eve.* What is birth?
> *The Serpent.* The serpent never dies. Some day you shall see me come out of this beautiful skin, a new snake with a new and lovelier skin. That is birth.
> *Eve.* I have seen that. It is wonderful.
> *The Serpent.* If I can do that, what can I not do? I tell you I am very subtle. When you and Adam talk, I hear you say "Why?" Always "Why?" You see things; and you say "Why?" But I dream things that never were; and I say "Why not?" I made the word dead to describe my old skin that I cast when I am renewed. I call that renewal being born.
> *Eve.* Born is a beautiful word.
> *The Serpent.* Why not be born again and again as I am, new and beautiful every time?
> *Eve.* I! It does not happen: that is why.
> *The Serpent.* That is how; but it is not why. Why not?... I dared everything. And at last I found a way of gathering together a part of the life in my body.
> *Eve.* What is life?
> *The Serpent.* That which makes the difference between the dead fawn and the live one.
> *Eve.* What a beautiful word! And what a wonderful thing! Life is the loveliest of all the new words.
> *The Serpent.* Yes: it was by meditating on Life that I gained the power to do miracles.
> *Eve.* Miracles? Another new word.
> *The Serpent.* A miracle is an impossible thing that is nevertheless possible. Something that never could happen, and yet does happen.
> *Eve.* Tell me some miracle that you have done.
> *The Serpent.* I gathered a part of the life in my body, and shut it into a tiny white case made of the stones I had eaten.

Eve. And what good was that?

The Serpent. I shewed the little case to the sun, and left it in its warmth. And it burst. And a little snake came out; and it became bigger and bigger from day to day until it was as big as I. That was the second birth.

Eve. Oh! That is too wonderful. It stirs inside me. It hurts.

In the Second Act, the language becomes heavy. It is suggestive of the burden of life that presses on the human race; the joy of living is gone. Instead of the sparkling dialogue of the first scene, Shaw now gives us a series of long rhetorical speeches, most eloquent of which are those of Cain. His defense of the murder of his brother and of his wild life is an impassioned speech consisting of pointed statements that startle us by their vigor. The rhetorical questions he brandishes have a compelling quality. Thus, speaks Cain:

Whose fault was it that I killed Abel? Who invented killing? Did I? No: he invented it himself. I followed your teaching. I dug and dug and dug. I cleared away the thistles and briars. I ate the fruits of the earth. I lived in the sweat of my brow, as you do. I was a fool. But Abel was a discoverer, a man of ideas, of spirit: a true Progressive. He was the discoverer of blood. He was the inventor of killing. He found out that the fire of the sun could be brought down by a dewdrop. He invented the altar to keep the fire alive. He changed the beasts he killed into meat by the fire on the altar. He kept himself alive by eating meat. His meal cost him a day's glorious health-giving sport and an hour's amusing play with the fire. You learnt nothing from him: you drudged and drudged, and dug and dug and dug, and made me do the same. I envied his happiness, his freedom. I despised myself for not doing as he did instead of what you did. He became so happy that he shared his meal with the Voice that had whispered all his inventions to him. He said that the Voice was the voice of the fire that cooked his food, and that the fire that could cook could also eat. It was true: I saw the fire consume the food on his altar. Then I, too, made an altar and offered my food on it, my grains, my roots, my fruit. Useless: nothing happened. He laughed at me; and then my great idea: why not kill him as he killed the beasts? I struck; and he died, just as they did. Then I gave up your silly drudging ways, and lived as he had lived, by the chase, by the killing, and by the fire. Am I not better than you? stronger, happier, freer?

This is prose glowing with the heat of poetry, moving with an irresistible rhythm that results from its arrangements of ideas into climaxes, and its harmonious combinations of forceful brevity with majestic balance.

Although Shaw employs the same device of the rhetorical speech in Part II, the arguments of the Barnabas Brothers do not possess half the charm of the discussions in the preceding part. The language fails to involve us now, because the subject has become limited to the narrow field of politics, the politics of Shaw's time at that. A vestige of Shaw's eloquence, however, remains in the speech of Franklyn explaining Adam's Fall: his deterioration in morale which was also the beginning of men's coming to think that their span of life should cover only what it does now.

When Shaw presents the thing as happening in Part III, the wit that enlivened Part I returns—a wit that spreads as humor, and at times as satire. Just as it had been The Serpent in First Act, now it is Confucius, the Chinese secretary of state, who becomes the mouthpiece of wit and epigrammatic statement; one feels that he is Shaw himself talking in the play with the clarity and irresistible force of the shrewd speaker. In answer to Burge-Lubin's claim that the English have on the whole managed to hold their own as a great race, Confucius remarks:

> I did not say you could do nothing. You could fight. You could eat. You could drink. Until the twentieth century you could produce children. You could play games. You could work when you were forced to. But you could not govern yourselves.

The inherent irony and satire of the speech is self-evident. Again it is Confucius who declares later,

> . . . Ever since I learnt to distinguish between one English face and another I have noticed what the woman pointed out: that the English face is not an adult face, just as the English mind is not an adult mind.

As the conversation goes on, it is easy to imagine Shaw stalking on the stage as Confucius, poking fun at Englishmen by thrusting his sharp-pointed witticisms at them.

Not even Shaw, however, can make the final parts interest an audience. Notwithstanding his eloquence and flashes of poetry, he cannot succeed in manipulating language sufficiently to arouse interest in subjects the audience feels too remote to deserve attention.

Nonetheless, the successful parts of *Back to Methuselah* demonstrate the efficiency of the language of immediacy—the language which can involve the audience by the very forcefulness of its familiar everyday accent used in discussion.

Judith: Stylized Debate

If the immediate appeal of *J. B.* and *Back to Methuselah* consists in providing the audience with a language that involves it in a discussion, that of Giraudoux's *Judith* and *Cantique de Cantiques* lies in their use of the language of debate. For one of "Giraudoux's most apparent devices is the presentation of stylized debates in which the characters embody the great themes in question."[6] *Judith* is organized around the debate between sensual love and saintliness; *Cantique de Cantiques*, around the love of a young man and that of an old man. *J. B.* makes its impact on the audience by the vigor of its language, *Back to Methuselah* by its eloquence. *Judith* and *Cantique de Cantiques* charm the listeners by the skirmish of words, the unexpected reserves of language, and reversals of conversational flow. It is *Judith* which I intend to consider here, as it provides a clear demonstration of Giraudoux's language of stylized debate.

The debate in *Judith* takes place in three movements: first, the argument to decide whether Judith is really the heroine chosen by God to deliver the Jews from the Assyrian General, Holofernes; second, the actual struggle between love of pleasure and devotion to a heroic mission; third, the debate on whether Judith was really the heroic saint presented in Scripture, or merely a pleasure-seeking woman.

All through the play, the language is characterized by concreteness of detail. The sparkle of words is directed to the imagination and to physical sensation rather than to the intellect. There is a clash of phrases with their sensuous suggestion. The dramatist arouses feelings that seem opposed to each other, only to conclude that there is no distinct borderline between them—they are coexistent rather than mutually exclusive.

The first act shows two groups of personages, each group flanking one side of the debate on the question of God's election of Judith. The Rabbis have ranged the townspeople on their side, from the prophets to the children, to declare that Judith has been so chosen to save Israel. On the other side stands Judith herself, Joseph her uncle, and Jean her lover.

---

6 Jacques Guicharnaud, *Modern French Theatre from Giraudoux to Beckett* (Yale University Press, 1961), p. 20.

The language of the first act is distinguished by scintillating live-liness. Joseph's angry skepticism rises in a crescendo reviling the prophets and the Rabbis for organizing the town in a campaign to involve Judith in a mission tearing her from her home, separating her from ordinary people by an act of heroism. The heated dialogue between Joseph and Joachim the Rabbi is succeeded by the refreshing talk of Judith. Like her uncle, she is on guard against the Rabbis, but her speech is disarmingly winsome. Hers is the language of the young woman free from inhibitions. The debate really ends in Judith's defeat when she gives vent to feelings of disgust for the weakness of the Jewish men, and decides that she is to be the strength of Israel that night. Judith the woman has given way to Judith the elect of God, a situation which she had been trying to parry from the start. However, the debate is prolonged in an attempt of the prostitute Suzanne to save Judith from an experience that would remove all the glory of her womanhood. It is Suzanne now who assumes the position that had formerly been Judith's. To Suzanne, what the elders envision as heroism for Judith would merely be the loss of her virginity which is her pride as a woman. Judith is unflinching, however, in her decision to be the heroine saint envisioned for her by the nation.

The second act presents a debate drawn from experience, showing in actuality how far she could struggle to abide by her decision. Two scenes are assigned to the debate between Judith and Holofernes, one symbolizing the supernatural mission, and the other the natural condi-tion of man: the woman called to sanctity, and the man calling her to pleasure. One feels no struggle, however, for very early in the scene, Judith is already on the side of Holofernes, and the presence of God has become something remote to her new condition. In answer to the voluptuous sensuousness of the speech of Holofernes, Judith melts into a tenderness from which awareness of guilt gradually recedes. Judith the Saint is lost; there remains only Judith the pleasure seeker. Holo-fernes has offered her the gifts that the natural man possesses:

> Do not despise such gifts. I offer you simplicity and calm for as long as you wish them. I offer you your childhood vocabulary, words concocted of the cherry and the grape in which you will fail to find God as in a glass. I offer you the musicians whom you will hear singing songs, not hymns. Their voice dies softly beneath them, around us; it is not raised to heaven

as a cry of terror. I offer you pleasure Judith. . . . Before this word of
tenderness, you will notice Jehovah vanishing. . . . (Act II, Sc. 4)[7]

In the monologue that ends the second act, Judith confides to the
reportedly deaf and dumb Daria, the woman sent to assist her; this is
her acceptance of the offering of Holofernes:

> He triumphs. . . . The affair of Judith will be sealed for him in a moment
> . . . What do you say? He is handsome? Yes, Holofernes is handsome,
> Daria. . . . This may well be the adventure of all those who have believed
> in themselves. . . .

Defeat has come to Judith. She had relied on her powers of eloquence;
asked what weapon she was bringing to defend herself against Holofernes, she answered:

> . . . My language. Man is a charlatan, Suzanne. . . . I have taken care of
> my voice, eating hardly anything. What I feel again is not the enthusiasm
> of a martyr, but an inexpressible urge for discourse, for arguments destined
> to prove I do not know what, except that I shall prove it. (Act I, Sc. 8)

The brilliance of her language displayed itself before Holofernes, only
to be smothered by his air of cool confidence in his own powers,
assurance of what a man can offer a woman.

The final debate in Act III takes place after Judith has slain
Holofernes. Her memory of the night gives the lie to the elders' claim
of the sanctity of her mission. With Judith proving her point beyond
all doubt, it is as if she has, as the Rabbi remarked, cut all the bridges
that lead to God (Act III, Sc. 6). To put Judith to death in the act of
proving that her night was not characterized by sanctity did not,
however, seem satisfactory to Giraudoux, and so, to get out of a blind
alley, he employs a "deus ex machina" in the form of the guardian
angel speaking through the medium of a guard. And henceforth, the
inconsistencies in the language begin. Giraudoux has been accused of a
"calculated irresponsibility." It is said that the most dreadful bathos
comes when Giraudoux threatens to relate his "amusing fancies" to a
series of serious positions, "to give them an axis, to take responsibility
for them."[8] We feel that this is exactly what the dramatist is doing at
the end of his *Judith*. He has drawn a Judith foreign to the Scriptures,

---

[7] Translations appearing on this page are mine.
[8] H. S. Mason, "Existentialism and Literature," *Scrutiny*, XIII: 1, p. 96.

and to justify his portrait he resorts to an unthinkable device. He makes the guardian angel talk as though deliberately making Judith live her night with Holofernes all over again. And yet, this angel succeeds in transforming the pleasure-loving Judith, in a few moments, into a woman who declares herself dried up of emotions and physical sensations. The young woman who had taken pride in her gift of language has no longer any arguments to offer. She accepts all the conditions laid down by the elders for her position as a saintly heroine despite her experience testifying to the contrary. The "angel" had convinced her that her night of sensual love had been a night of sanctity at one and the same time, but her language points to the contrary. For Judith "the Saint" no longer speaks with the vigor that belongs to her; yet, neither does her speech rise with the exaltation of the soul that is really possessed by God.

The battle of words that makes up the debate in *Judith* possesses partial immediacy that takes an audience in certain scenes. But it fails to do so ultimately because artistic unity is disrupted by the disharmony of the language in its totality, which arouses suspicion that somewhere in the play, the structure is out of joint.

THE VOICE OF THE POET

The use of a language that possesses immediate appeal to the audience has its own rewards. But to convey the sense of mystery which is necessary in order to do full justice to the biblical theme, dramatists have seen the advantages of employing language that can communicate a kind of double pattern. While grasping the surface meaning of the characters' words, the audience is made aware of another plane of meaning suggested by the language itself. According to T.S. Eliot, it is poetic drama that can give the impression of "a kind of doubleness in the action, as if it took place on two planes at once."[9] For it is in the nature of poetry to be capable of holding a wealth of meaning, something which is beyond prose.

In considering the three dramas in this section, it is my aim to study the varying effects produced by the dramatist through the poetry of their language.

---

9 "John Marston," *Select Essays,* p. 229.

Lazarus Laughed: The Rhythm of Enchantment

According to Nietzsche, "Enchantment is the precondition of all dramatic art."[10] *Lazarus Laughed* is evidently O'Neill's attempt to embody the ideas that Nietzsche expounded in *The Birth of Tragedy from the Spirit of Music;* the distinctive feature of the play is the atmosphere of enchantment that pervades it. This can be said to be the result of a harmonious blending of spectacle and language.

In studying the language of *Lazarus Laughed*, we shall start with a classification of the characters into three key groups that determine the speech used: (1) the hero and the characters who really hold a dialogue with him: Lazarus and Miriam, Tiberius Caesar, Caligula; (2) the crowds who comment, argue and wrangle, portraying changing moods; (3) the chorus whose chanting pervades the atmosphere of the play. Because it is with the chorus that each scene is generally begun and ended, we shall start with a consideration of the role of its incantations.

With the exception of the two scenes in Act IV, each of the other scenes in the play opens with a choral chant. As the curtain rises and the audience beholds the setting of the scene, the chorus in masks intones its recitation which becomes the keynote of the scene—the soul, so to speak, giving the undercurrent to the action. In the first scene of Act I, the key words of the chorus are:

> He that liveth
> He that believeth
> Shall never die!

The choral ending of the same scene enumerates all the laughing accompaniments of Lazarus' laughter, in nature:

> Lazarus laughs!
> Our hearts grow happy!
> Laughter like music!
> The wind laughs!
> The sea laughs!
> Spring laughs from the earth!
> Summer laughs in the air!
> Lazarus laughs!

---

10 Friedrich Nietzsche, *op. cit.*, p. 300.

There is a cumulative effect in the lines, a swelling to the final paean of the closing chorus of Scene One:

> Laugh! Laugh!
> Fear is no more!
> There is no death!
> Laugh! Laugh!
> There is only life
> There is only laughter
> Fear is no more!
> Death is dead!
> Laugh! Laugh!
> Death is dead!
> There is only laughter!

And the dramatist writes, "The room rocks, the air outside throbs with the rhythmic beat of their liberated laughter—still a bit uncertain of its freedom, harsh, discordant, frenzied, desperate and drunken, but dominated and inspired by the high, free, aspiring, exulting laughter of Lazarus." It is extremely difficult to imagine the language apart from the rhythm which is what gives power to the utterance in simple, hypnotic, repetitive lines. These lines are carried on to the beginning of the next scene at the end of which we hear the cry of bewilderment when Lazarus' followers witness the number of people who die in the violence of clashing mobs, while the Centurion announces his orders to bring Lazarus to Rome. The disciples of the laughing leader, once rapturous laughers themselves, now huddle together and cry:

> Death slinks out
> Of his grave in the heart!
> Ghosts of fear
> Creep back in the brain!
> We remember fear!
> We remember death.
>
> Death in the heart!
> Fear in the brain!
> We remember fear!
> We remember death!
> Forgotten is laughter!
> We remember
> Only death.
> Fear is God!
> Forgotten is laughter!
> Life is death!

Life is a fearing,
A long dying,
From birth to death!
God is a slayer!
Life is death!

At the beginning of the first scene in Act II, the chorus of Greeks intones its words of expectation:

Soon the God comes!
Redeemer and Savior!
Dionysus, Son of Man and a God!

Midway in the scene, as Lazarus approaches, the chorus chants in "a deep rhythmic monotone like the rising and falling cadences of waves on a beach":

He comes, the Redeemer and Savior!
Laughing along the mountains
To give back our lost laughter
To raise from the dead our freedom
To free us from Rome!

And the crowd takes up the cry:

Fireborn! Redeemer! Savior!
Raise from the dead our freedom!
Give back our lost laughter!
Free us from Rome!

The tension between the Roman soldiers and the crowd they are trying to restrain results in a fierce chorus of "Death," stirring both sides to strike. It is at this moment that the voice of Lazarus "comes ringing through the air like a command from the sky," and as he appears his words are:

There is no death!

Hearing this the soldiers and Greeks remain "frozen in their attitudes of murderous hate" until the sound of his laughter fills them with "the sheepish shame of children caught in mischief" and "their hands hang, their arms sink to their sides." (p. 414) And once more the chorus of followers chants the leitmotif of the play:

Laugh! Laugh!
There is no death!

> There is only life!
> There is only laughter!

And the Dionysiac enthusiasm for Lazarus rises once more.

At the beginning, the Chorus of the Senate in the second scene, laid in Rome, intones wearily as if under boring compulsion, conveying the keynote of fatigue in struggle, giving the audience a foreboding of the death of many of Lazarus' followers singing

> Laugh! Laugh! Laugh!
> Death is dead!
> Dead! Dead! Dead!

There is a heaviness in the sound of their chanting as many of them then fall dead.

In the two scenes of Act III laid in the exterior of Tiberius Caesar's villa palace at Capri, the chorus, consisting of the guards in double masks and gorgeous uniforms and armor, stands in silence. The weirdness of the scene demands silence as more fitting than a chant—a silence that inspires a fearful foreboding. The first scene repeats the choral ending of the preceding Act, whereas the second scene closes with the hysterical laughter of the chorus anticipating Lazarus' death:

> Ha-ha-ha-ha! Ha-ha-ha-ha!
> Let us die, Lazarus!
> Mercy, Laughing One!
> Mercy of death!
> Ha-ha-ha-ha! Ha-ha-ha-ha!

Neither of the two scenes in Act IV begin with a choral chant. They end, however, with a more hopeful note than the scenes of Act III. Seeing Lazarus lifting the dead body of his wife Miriam, and hearing him laugh softly and tenderly, the chorus whispers:

> That is it!
> Love is pure!
> Love is tender!
> Laugh!

And the crowd echoes: "Laugh! Laugh!"

At the end of the play, the dramatist elaborates on the leitmotif, and makes the chorus chant as it dances listening to the laughter of the dying Lazarus:

Laugh! Laugh!
We are stars!
We are dust!
We are gods!
We are laughter!
We are dust!
We are gods!
Laugh! Laugh!

The implication in these final lines of the chorus is that men, though dying, have in them the power of divinity to rise again to life. Hence, laughter—joy, not sorrow—should accompany their acceptance of life.

An analysis of the chorus in *Lazarus Laughed* reveals the major role assigned to it by the dramatist. And yet, the poetry sung by the chorus is by itself but the second voice in poetry according to T.S. Eliot—the voice of the poet speaking to an audience. The choral lines contain the message which the playwright wishes to convey; they do not promote the action proper in the play. This role is performed by the individuals from the crowd who propose conflicting opinions, at times echoing the chorus, but often contradicting it. Opposition to Lazarus develops the agony in each scene in which the hero merely responds with his multicolored laughter, expressing the eternal, reproving the earthly, and giving strength to his followers.

It is worthwhile noticing that whereas the choral lines are all in verse, the dialogues carried on by individuals in the crowd are always in prose, except when voices are formed to swell the prevailing cry of the chorus.

If the choral lines are idealistic, the passages spoken by individuals in the crowd are characterized by realistic concreteness of detail, the tang of everyday speech. Talking about Lazarus, as people do at a wake, the guests recall the circumstances before his death:

> Third Guest. (a Self-Tortured Man—gloomily) Yes, of late years his life had been one long misfortune. One after another his children died—
> Sixth Guest. (A Mature Man with a cruel face—with a harsh laugh) They were all girls. Lazarus had no luck.
> Seventh Guest. The last was a boy, the one that died at birth. You are forgetting him.
> Third Guest. Lazarus could never forget. Not only did his son die but Miriam could never bear him more children. (p. 384)

The displeasure with Lazarus and his laughing followers is expressed by the aged Jew who bewails the neglect of work on his farm: "That loafer taught them that! They come to him and work for nothing! for nothing! And they are glad, these undutiful ones! While they sow, they dance! They sing to the earth when they are plowing! They tend his flocks and laugh toward the sun! Ha-ha-ha!" (p. 395).

In Act II, one of the individuals in the waiting crowd speaks of the influence Lazarus is said to have on people:

> First Greek. Does he truly resemble a god?
>
> Fourth Greek. One look in his eyes while his laughter sings in your ears and you forget sorrow! You dance! You laugh! It is as if a heavy weight you had been carrying all your life without knowing it suddenly were lifted. You are a cloud, you can fly, your mind reels with laughter, you are drunk with joy! (Solemnly) Take my word for it, he is indeed a god. Everywhere the people have acclaimed him. He heals the sick, he raises the dead, by laughter.
>
> Seventh Greek. But I have heard that when he has gone people cannot remember his laughter, that the dead are dead again and the sick die, and the sad grow more sorrowful.
>
> Fifth Greek. Well, we shall soon see with our own eyes. But why should the God return in the body of a Jew? (p. 408)

The crowds speak in prose apparently intended to be that of everyday life. One might imagine Lazarus speaking in verse, too, since his words are the elaboration of the leitmotif intoned and repeated in the choral verses. Yet, the hero invariably speaks in prose except in short lines which are but restatements of the leitmotif. Nonetheless, his prose is highly rhetorical and often rises to the level of poetry.

Except in his dialogues with the major characters with whom he really has rapport, like Miriam, Tiberius and Caligula, Lazarus' speech is the voice of the poet talking to an audience—the chorus and the crowds included. His utterance is that of the seer, generally epigrammatic, with sufficient obscurity to allow for ambiguity of meaning, so that one is aware of more than one level of interpretation. If one follows his eloquent speeches, however, one discovers the leitmotif expressed in several varying shades, elaborated on and made to appeal by the rise and fall of their inherent rhythms. The key lines to the speeches as given below will show what is meant by the preceding statements.

	KEY LINES Spoken by Lazarus	IDEAS EXPRESSED
ACT I, Sc. 1: (p. 387)	There is only life.... And my heart reborn to love of life cried "yes!" And I laughed in the laughter of God.	—Affirmation of life —God's life as joy
ACT I, Sc. 2: (p. 397)	Men's tragedy is to forget the god in them. The greatness of Man is that no god can save him—until he becomes a god.	—To rise to the joy of God is to become a god.
ACT II, Sc. 1: (p. 417)	But as dust you are eternal change and everlasting growth, and a high note of laughter soaring through chaos from the deep heart of God.	—Man as part of nature undergoes eternal recurrence: change from one state to another.
(p. 418)	Man must learn to live by laughter.	—Sharing in God's joy.
ACT II, Sc. 2: (p. 432)	He must conceive and desire his own passing as a mood of eternal laughter and cry with pride, "Take back, O God and accept in turn a gift from me, my grateful blessing for Your gift—and see, O God, now I am laughing with You! I am Your laughter—and You are mine!	—Man must accept death as a mood of eternal joy, and offer it to God.
ACT III, Sc. 1: (p. 438)	There is God's laughter on the hills of space and the happiness of children, and the soft healing of innumerable dawns and evenings, and the blessing of peace.	—The only reality is God's joy seen in children and in nature—a reality with the blessing of peace.
ACT III, Sc. 2: (p. 449)	There is no death, Caesar. There is only life ... and laughter.	—Affirmation of life and joy
ACT IV, Sc. 1: (p. 467)	If you can answer Yes to pain there is no pain.	—Affirmation of life removes pain ... there is only joy
(p. 469)	Go out under the sky! Let your heart climb on laughter to a star.	—Active affirmation of life; elevation of the spirit through joy
(p. 472)	Love has grown purer! The laughter of God is more profoundly tender!	—Death is a purification of love—the

IDEAS EXPRESSED

experience of God's
tender joy.

ACT IV, Sc. 2:	(What is beyond there, Lazarus?)	—Final restatement
(p. 477)	Life! Eternity! Stars and dust! God's	of Eternal Recur-
	Eternal Laughter!	rence in nature
		through God's joy

There is no complicated logic in the lines uttered by Lazarus. The arrangement of words is simple but melodious—stirring the heart by their cadence. To the crowds, Lazarus is a teacher with a message. Among the few characters who at certain moments hold rapport with the hero is his wife, Miriam, to whom the tenderest passages are assigned. In Scene Two of the second Act, knowing that if she eats the peach offered by Pompeia she must die, she reviews her life of love for Lazarus. There is something nostalgic in her last speech:

> (bites into the peach and, chewing, begins, as if immediately affected, to talk like a garrulous old woman, her words coming quicker and quicker as her voice becomes fainter and fainter) Say what you like, it is much better I should go home first, Lazarus. We have been away so long, there will be so much to attend to about the house. And all the children will be waiting. You would be as helpless as a child, Lazarus. Between you and the children, things would soon be in a fine state! (More and more confused) No, no! You cannot help me, dearest one. You are only in my way. No, I will make the fire. When you laid it the last time, we all had to run for our lives, choking, the smoke poured from the windows, the neighbors thought the house was burning! (She laughs—a queer, vague little inward laugh) You are so impractical. The neighbors all get the best of you. Money slips through your fingers. If it was not for me—(She sighs—then brightly and lovingly) But, dearest husband, why do you take it so to heart? Why do you feel guilty because you are not like other men? That is why I love you so much. ... Even if God has taken our little ones—yes, in spite of sorrow—have you not a good home I make for you, and a wife who loves you? (She forces a chuckle) Be grateful, then—for me! Smile, my sad one! Laugh a little once in a while! Come home, bringing me laughter of the wind from the hills! (Swaying, looking at the peach in her hand) What a mellow, sweet fruit! Did you bring it home for me? (She falls back into his arms.) pp. 453-54.

Some of the lines spoken by her can be considered to complement those of Lazarus, as when she says, "Is it a sin to be born a dreamer?

But God, He must be a dreamer, too, or how would we be on earth?"
(p. 454)

Totally unlike Miriam's are the words of other outstanding characters such as Tiberius, Pompeia and Caligula. At certain moments,
a breath of tenderness comes even to the first two, hardened though
they are by habitual distrust in the court. But on the whole, their
speech conveys the jarring notes releasing the countermovement in the
rhythm, only to blend into harmony with Lazarus' utterance at the end.
Even Caligula's final words, characterized though they are by sharp
countermovements, end with a note of sympathy for the hero. Having
killed both Tiberius and Lazarus, Caligula behaves like a madman.
"Groveling in a paroxysm of terror," he hears Lazarus' last words:
"Fear not, Caligula! There is not death!" and he rises with childish
laughter on his lips, saying:

> I laugh, Lazarus! I laugh with you! (Then grief-stricken) Lazarus! (He
> hides his face in his hands, weeping) No more! (Then beats his head
> with his fists) I will remember! I will! (Then suddenly, with a return to
> grotesqueness—harshly) All the same, I killed him and I proved there is
> death! (Immediately overcome by remorse, groveling and beating himself)
> Fool! Madman! Forgive me, Lazarus! Men forget!

A mixture of prose and verse, *Lazarus Laughed* is nonetheless
poetic drama. It possesses to an eminent degree one of the aspects
of poetry as defined by Ezra Pound: "(1) Melopoeia, to wit, poetry
which moves by its music, whether it be music in words or an aptitude
for, or suggestion of accompanying music."[11] The highly melodious
poetry of the play opens up visions of the possibilities of eternal
recurrence.

One might say that *Lazarus Laughed* abounds in the "second
voice—the voice of the poet addressing an audience." In dealing with
drama, however, we naturally expect to find a predominance of the
"third voice—the voice of the poet when he attempts to create a
dramatic character speaking in verse; when he is saying, not what he
would say in his own person, but only what he can say within the
limits of one imaginary character."[12] Yet, we hear this third voice

---

[11] From a review of "Others: An Anthology." *Little Review,* March 1918;
quoted by D. E. Maxwell in *The Poetry of T.S. Eliot* (London: Routledge &
Kegan Paul, 1961), p. 13.

[12] T.S. Eliot, *On Poetry and Poets* (New York: The Noonday Press, 1961),
p. 96.

only in dialogues between Lazarus and those characters who have real rapport with him. Even then we sense that the rhythm in their utterance is somehow designed to blend with the music of the whole which is the unifying element in the piece.

The difference in tone between the chanting of the chorus and Lazarus' inspired speeches on the one hand, and the realistic speech of the crowds and that of the characters voicing opposition on the other, makes the drama move on two levels, with the effect of giving the audience a sense of mystery befitting a biblical theme, notwithstanding the fact that *Lazarus Laughed* is not in accord with the biblical spirit in the orthodox interpretation. The banter, the wrangle and the heated verbal skirmishes among individuals of the crowd make us aware of the temporary—the world where changes affect people, moving them to sorrow or to passionate resistance. The choruses, on the whole, together with Lazarus, put us in touch with a sphere where, in the design of eternal recurrence, even painful events are viewed as elements that can be congruous with the laughter of God.

This awareness of the temporal and the eternal is effected by O'Neill's ability to build up an atmosphere of mystery dominated by a music in which dialogue forms an integral part.

A Sleep of Prisoners—The Logic of Dream Language

In mulling over the meaning that he saw in the life of soldiers, Christopher Fry must have been confronted by the problem of reconciling the exalted nature of the biblical material with the informal tone that soldiers take in their everyday language. The idea of presenting the soldiers' night in a sequence of dreams has solved the problem admirably, resulting in what Derek Stanford describes as the impression of a new category in religious drama,[13] for the contrast between the language of the soldiers in their waking moments and their language when dreaming produces an impact upon the audience, making it feel as though listening not merely to the individual stripped of all disguises, but also to humanity speaking through the ages.

Joe Adams awakes, speaks casually, with some touch of humor, alive to actuality. Inquiring about Meadows' ailment, he says, "How's

---

[13] Derek Stanford, *Christopher Fry, An Appreciation* (London: Peter Nevill Ltd., 1951), p. 204.

the leg feel, Meadows?"[14] Imitating the enemy officer's talk when he brought them to the church building that was to serve as their prison, he says,

> You heard the towzer Commandant:
> 'All more buildings blow up into sky,
> No place like home now. Roof here, good and kind
> To prisoners. Keep off sun, keep off rain.' (p. 2)

To which Peter Able adds: "Keep off grass" in obvious parody.

In sleep, the language of Adams becomes symbolic. In the dream figure of Adam in Genesis, watching his sons' rivalry, he exclaims:

> Look, sir, my sons are playing.
> How silent the spectators are,
> World, air, and water.
> Eyes bright, tension, halt.
> Still as a bone from here to the sea. (p. 14)

In these lines, the universe itself is watching the two sons of Adam contesting with each other to prove who would be stronger in spirit. And we are conscious that there are really more witnesses to the contest—God Himself, the spirits of light and the spirits of darkness. The first brothers have become the center of the universe, and their deeds, a drama engaging the attention of onlookers beyond the family circle. The language spoken by the dream figure of Adam is fraught with a tension which cannot be found in the waking speech of Corporal Adams.

Still further on, at the end of the dream sequence, Adams speaks as man himself baffled by the doings of men. The lines:

> Strange how we trust the powers that ruin
> And not the powers that bless. (p. 48)

can be read as a comment on the ways of nations that use their resources for the armaments destined to break the efforts of men through the centuries, rather than for channeling their energies toward peaceful purposes.

Through the dream language in *A Sleep of Prisoners,* Fry has taken up the questions posed by soldiers as well as by all who are

---

[14] Oxford University Press edition, 1959, p. 2.

involved in war, and he has tried to give possible answers through the speech of various dream figures. In this drama, war is the problem not only of the four soldiers but also of humanity itself. War has been the problem of men through the centuries. The dramatist conceived of the ages in history as background to his drama; this is the leitmotif that runs through the whole play. To David's question while still awake, "How long are we here for?" meaning, how long are they to be in prison, Adams jokingly replies, "A million years." (p. 9). Later on, in a dream, Peter asks, "What nightmare's this you're dragging me into?" To which Adams answers, "Humanity's." (p. 24). In the last dream, Meadows asks, "Who will trust what the years have endlessly said?" He himself makes the subsequent statement, "Behind us lie/The thousand, and the thousand and the thousand years/Vexed and terrible. And still we use/The cures which never cure." (p. 47). Evidently, Fry wishes to convey the agelessness of the problem of war. His comment seems to be that we never learn from history, but despite the lesson it teaches, nations resort to war as if violence could bring about peace.

By the dream language in which the bosom of each of the four prisoners is stripped bare, they voice the questions which every soldier is bound to ask, the questions that come as a groan from a humanity that is oppressed by war. The first question is implied in Peter Able's lines when speaking as Isaac:

> Surely there's no need for us to be
> The prisoners of the dark? Smile, father.
> Let me go. (p. 32)

Why should men be soldiers? Why should there be a war? The last line, "Let me go," expresses the wish deep in the heart of the soldier to be freed from war in order to go and live his own life. David's reply is a statement of the answer of the nations who engage in war— the answer of the families who must send their loved sons to war:

> Against my heart
> I let you go, for the world's own ends
> I let you go, for God's will
> I let you go, for children's children's joy
> I let you go, my grief obeying.
> The cords bind you against my will
> But you're bound for a better world.

> And I must lay you down to sleep
> For a better waking. (p. 32)

In these words, Fry sums up the logic of nations who go to war. Unless soldiers realized that they are going through the agonizing experience of war, "For our better freedom/Which makes us living men" (p. 31), they would not allow themselves to be dragged into the nightmare. It is an idealism that makes them believe that they should lay down their lives for a better world.

Despite this ideal, however, soldiers plunged in the horrors of war find it hard to grasp the meaning of their existence. "Who are we, Dave, who/Are we?" exclaims Adams in anguish. "If we could know who we are—" (p. 42). The answer comes later when Dave cries, "Tied hand and foot: not men at all!" As prisoners, they find that their activities are not those of men. Their care is how to think the moments out "Before thinking splits to fear." Asked to stand at attention, they find that they cannot do it, their hands being tied. Commanded to stand at ease, they are incapable of doing it, for their feet, too, are tied. And Adams realizes, "That leaves me without a word of command/Except fall on your knees" (p. 43). The experience of war has made the prisoners aware of the presence of a power greater than they, before whom they kneel. Amazed at being able to survive the flames, Adams exclaims:

> What way have I come down, to find
> I live still, in this round of blaze?
> Here on my knees. And a fire hotter
> Than any fire has ever been
> Plays over me. And I live. I know
> I kneel. . . .
> We're not destroyed. (p. 44)

They find the answer to the question that had been posed by Adams. It is David who declares, "We're men who sleep and wake." This is what Fry thinks of soldiers: they are men who sleep through the nightmare of war, and wake to a realization of their relationship to the Invisible Power. And war is the monster that exists "To make sure we know eternity's in earnest" (p. 41). The experience of helplessness in the midst of danger shocks soldiers out of confidence in their own power, bringing them face to face with Him from whom all power comes. The threat of death enables them to think of death and of the life after death, so that men who had hardly given thought to eternity come to grips with it, and get ready to plunge into this hitherto unthought of sphere. What had formerly been a vague idea becomes, through war, a vivid reality.

The next question Fry puts in the mouth of Adams is, "May we come through?" (p. 46) And Meadows answers: "If you have the patience and the love." Earlier in the play, Adams had discovered, "I can think of life. We'll make it yet" (p. 45). The question does not merely mean, "Can we survive the experience of war? Can we live through these flames?" It also implies the doubt of being able to survive the agony, so that after living lives that can hardly be called human, they would still retain their qualities as men. The answer of Meadows is conditional: the experience of war is such that to go through it chastened, people must have the patience and the love that will transform mere men into beings that are "more than men" (p. 40), men initiated into the divine secrets of eternity.

It is difficult to conceive another method by which Fry could have achieved as much as in *A Sleep of Prisoners*. In his use of dreams in the structure of his drama, Fry has been preceded by such dramatists as James Barrie and Bernard Shaw. In *A Kiss for Cinderella*, the former makes the heroine, Jane, dream in the figure of her archetype, the poor girl who wins her prince charming. In *Man and Superman*, Shaw conceives of a scene from the simultaneous dream of two characters in the play. Fry has proceeded a step further, making all the characters in his play dream the same dream simultaneously, each in a different dream figure, so that Old Testament episodes are enacted by them. Moreover, in the plays of Barrie and Shaw, there is hardly any difference in language between the characters in their waking hours and in their dreams, showing that although the characters dream in their archetypal figures, their dreams are merely projections of their personal unconscious,[15] even though influenced by their respective knowledge of literature. In *A Sleep of Prisoners*, the characters do not merely dream in their archetypal figures, they also speak from the

---

15 Froeda Fordham, *An Introduction to Jung's Psychology* (Penguin Books, 1954), p. 47: "These repressed tendencies belong to what Jung calls the personal unconscious . . ."

collective unconscious,[16] so that what they say in sleep surpasses what they are able to say as individuals in their waking hours, their words coming from the wisdom of humanity acquired through the centuries. For, what one would hesitate to say in his waking hours, aware as he is of his situation as an individual, he can say with eloquence when the energy is released from his collective unconsciousness in sleep.

Despite the fact that Fry's method can be justified by the psychology of dreams, the dramatist's role as choreographer of the dreams is evident. His pattern in *A Sleep of Prisoners* is indeed a highly sophisticated one. But in following this pattern and giving it the interior of a church for a background, Fry has succeeded in bringing over to his audience his insight into the meaning of the life of soldiers. The idea of presenting prisoners in a nightmare is highly effective in its symbolism. For the experience of war is a nightmare from which those who wake and return to everyday life, away from the battlefield, can come to a realization of the meaning of life as they had never done before.

In this efficient handling of the illogical material of dreams, Fry has succeeded in attaining a logic of dream language that surpasses that of consciousness.

The Personalization of Biblical Language

Stanislas Fumet has come near the truth when he wrote that Claudel arrived at the melody of his verses through his constant listening to the voice of the liturgy.[17] And what is the liturgy but the Bible as used in worship? Of all the dramas of Claudel, there is not one which breathes the spirit of the Bible, as revealed in the liturgy, as much as *L'Annonce faite à Marie*. In this drama, the theme which finds its roots in the Bible shoots forth foliage that thrives in the lives of the characters. For the beauty of the poetry in *L'Annonce* consists in the merging of biblical images with the spirit of the personages, in such a way that their allusions to the Bible become a revelation of

---

16 *Ibid.*, p. 23: "There are complexes which belong to the personal unconscious, and others which belong to the collective unconscious, a realm of the psyche that is common to all mankind."

17 Introduction to Paul Claudel: *Oeuvre Poetique,* by Stanislas Fumet (Gallimard, 1957), p. xxxii.

the life they live within. Each of these characters has been so nourished by the liturgy that references to the Bible form the very tissue of speech in moments of intensity. Thus, like Claudel himself, each of the characters in *L'Annonce* speaks biblical language with a spontaneity which is as unstudied as the act of breathing.

Even the speech of Mara who stands for evil in the play savors of the Bible, but only to betray the perversion of her spirit. When she finds it difficult to attain her goal of marriage with Jacques, she frightens her mother with words that recall the despair of Judas: "I'll hang myself in the woodshed."[18] At the time when she has recourse to her leprous sister at Chevoche, her echo of Violaine's words has the ring of irony: "So, He's with you, little dove, and He loves you?" Yet, while being ironical, she is using an image drawn from the biblical love canticle known as *The Song of Songs*.[19] Comparing the images in each situation in greater detail brings out the grotesqueness in Mara's remark. For the bride in *The Song of Songs* "hiding in the clefts of the rock, in the coverts of the cliff," is desirable in her beauty so that she is asked by the bridegroom to come out and show herself, whereas Violaine, ostracized as a leper, is condemned to conceal the hideousness of her person behind rocks and in the cavern of Chevoche. Mara's meaning hidden beneath the biblical phrasing is later made clear by her stinging assertion, "He has punished you hard." But the character of Mara can best be seen as the mixture of faith and violence at the final scene when she repeats the lines of the Angelus recited by her father: "And the Word was made flesh and dwelt among us..."[20] only to assert that it was her violence that had drawn the answer of God to her prayers, making her child live again.[21]

Jacques, too, can speak in the poetry of the Bible, despite his statement, "Heaven is for the heavenly, and earth for the earthly."

---

18 Cf. Matthew xxvi: "And casting down the pieces of silver in the temple, he departed and went and hanged himself with a halter."

19 *Theatre II*, p. 190: "Il est avec toi, petite colombe, Il t'aime?"

Cf. *The Song of Songs*, 2:13-14: Come, then, my love, my lovely one, come. My dove, hiding in the clefts of the rock, in the coverts of the cliff, show me your face, let me hear your voice, for your voice is sweet and your face is beautiful.

20 John 1:14.

21 *Theatre II*, p. 210-11. Cf. Matt. xi, 12: The kingdom of heaven suffers violence and the violent bear it away.

A farmer accustomed to watch the seed he has planted grow and bear fruit finds it difficult to see beyond the world of the senses. The beauty of Violaine, however, rouses him to a greeting similar to that of the spouse in *The Song of Songs:* "O my beloved among the branches in flower, hail!"[22] To him, man of the soil, Violaine possesses the beauty of the lily which he cannot tire of contemplating.[23] And when he comes to know that Violaine is afflicted with the fatal disease of leprosy which, simple man as he is, he believes to be a punishment of guilty love, he conveys his disappointment with a biblical allusion: "Such is the angel whom God has sent me," the reference evidently being to the angel whom God had given the young Tobias to accompany him on his long journey.[24]

Prosaic though the mother is, her speech is tinged with the color of biblical poetry in the agony of parting. To her husband who proposes to leave for Jerusalem she says, "I shall not let thee go,"[25] echoing the words of *The Song of Songs* once more. Violaine, whom she feels she will not see again and whom she suspects to be making an oblation in favor of Mara, she calls "my sacrificial lamb," recalling the image used by John the Baptist of Christ.[26] There is, in Violaine, the character of victim which the mother cannot but notice. The implication is that, like Christ, the Lamb of God, who offered Himself as a sacrifice for the world, Violaine will be offering her life for others.

If there is any character in the play whose situation could be most similar to that of Claudel himself, it is Pierre de Craon. And yet, the words spoken are in character—they belong to Pierre de Craon as much as to Claudel. The biblical images that Pierre uses are those picked out by a man who, while striving for sanctity, has experienced the violent and humiliating temptation of the flesh occasioned by none other than the pure Violaine. As he bids farewell to the maid on whom he has attempted to lay hands, he calls her, "O young tree of the

---

22 *Theatre II,* p. 167. Cf. *The Song of Songs,* V, 1: I am come into my garden, O my sister, my spouse.

23 *Ibid.,* p. 169. Non, mon beau lys, je ne puis me lasser de te considérer dans ta gloire!

24 *Ibid.,* p. 174. See *Tobit,* V-XII.

25 *Ibid.,* p. 151: Je ne t'en délierai pas.

Cf. *The Song of Songs,* III, 4: When I had a little passed by then I found him whom my soul loveth. I held him: and I would not let him go.

26 *Ibid.,* p. 180: Songe à cela, mon agneau sacrifié . . .

Cf. John I, 36: And beholding Jesus walking, he saith, Behold the Lamb of God.

knowledge of good and evil...,"[27] an allusion to the admonition Yahweh has given to Adam in the second account of the creation. In Pierre's case, Violaine is the instrument for him to discover the evil in himself, as well as the means of confirming him in his resolution to serve God for life as a builder of churches. Seeing in Violaine the image of the Eternal Beauty [28] which has attracted him, he realizes that he is not fated to be her partner in the home, for as an instrument of God, he is to be wedded to the church he builds, the life companion drawn from his side during his sleep of sorrow.[29] Pierre de Craon is the holy man whose sanctity is obtained at the cost of a painful struggle with the tendencies of the flesh: The poetry of his words welded into the language of Genesis leaves an unforgettable image of holiness and human weakness of the sinner who endeavors to be a saint. In presenting Pierre de Craon, Claudel consistently used images found in Genesis. Pierre is another Adam who is attracted to Violaine in whom he sees an image of Eternal Beauty. His admiration for her becomes an obsession, and trying to touch her, he finds that she is not only the fruit forbidden to him but also the tree of the knowledge of good and evil. Coming across her makes him recognize God's image in her beauty, but trying to touch her makes him aware of the evil in himself. The sickness of leprosy which he has contracted further makes him realize that she is not meant for him. He understands that in place of Violaine, other Eves would issue from his heart: the churches which he is to build for God.

It is Anne Vercors, Violaine's father, who is the raissoneur of the play, unveiling the meaning of his daughter's life in all its splendor. In journeying to Jerusalem, he has answered what he thought to be a call of God, marching along in spirit with members of the Church with whom, he firmly believes, he is in communion,[30] and he comes

---

27 *Ibid.*, p. 137. O jeune arbre de la science du Bien et du Mal . . .
   Cf. Genesis II, 17: But of the tree of the knowledge of good and evil, thou shalt not eat.
   28 *Ibid.*, p. 143: O image de la Beauté éternelle . . .
   Cf. Genesis I, 26: Let us make man to our image and likeness. . . .
   29 *Ibid.*, p. 144: Cette église seule sera ma femme qui va être tirée de mon coté comme une Ève de pierre dans le sommeil de la douleur.
   Cf. Genesis II, 21-22: And the Lord God built the rib which he took from Adam into a woman.
   30 *Ibid.*, pp. 151-52: Je ne suis pas seul! Les voilà tous en marche avec moi toutes ces âmes, les uns qui me poussent et les autres qui m'entraînent et les autres qui me tiennent la main.
   Cf. 1 Cor. XIII, 27: For in one Spirit were we all baptized into one body,

back to find Violaine in her death agony. At this moment, it is he
who dispels the suspicion that has been created through the years
regarding Violaine. He reveals her as the handmaid of the Lord, who,
like Mary, had pronounced her "Fiat!"[31] whereupon the sacrifice
demanded of her had borne fruit for a suffering Christendom. The
call which he had heard and which Violaine had responded to was
the same, but Violaine's answer was the better one. It was Violaine
who had realized the words that Pierre de Craon had spoken to her:
"Holiness doesn't come from being stoned by the Turks or kissing
a leper on his mouth, but by keeping the commandment of God,
whether it means staying in our own place or mounting higher."
(p. 141)

The core of the poetry in *L'Annonce*, nonetheless, is Violaine,
whose lines make up a masterpiece the beauty of which is drawn
from the Bible. In the biblical allusions found in her speech, we
notice how Claudel builds up an unmistakable image of her. For his
vision of Violaine is that of another Mary, fairest among women who,
in her purity of heart, has been chosen by God for the role of suffering
victim. Like Christ, who, after intense spiritual and physical suffering,
rises and greets His apostles with the peace which surpasses all understanding, Violaine breathes that peace which comes only from one
who is certain of the life after death. When Jacques becomes incon-
solable at the thought of having been instrumental in bringing about
her lifetime of suffering and her tragic death, her comforting words are
a paraphrase of Christ's assuring us of His victory over death.[32]

The message of the play is fittingly spoken by Violaine: "Suffer
with Christ," she reminds Pierre de Craon at the Prologue. And
at the end of the play, commenting on Jacques' hopelessness, she
declares:

---

whether Jews or Gentiles, whether bond or free. . . . Now you are the body of
Christ and members of member.

    [31] *Ibid.*, p. 207: L'Ange de Dieu a annoncé à Marie et elle a concu de
l'Esprit-Saint . . .Toute la grande douleur de ce monde autour d'elle, et l'Église
coupée en deux, et la France pour qui Jeanne a été brulée vive, elle l'a vue! Et
c'est pourquoi elle a baisé ce lepreux, sur la bouche, sachant ce qu'elle faisait.
    Cf. Luke 1:38: And Mary said: Behold the handmaid of the Lord: be it
done to me according to thy word.
    [32] *Ibid.*, p. 213: Dis, qu'est-ce qu'un jour loin de moi? Bientôt il sera passé.
Et alors quand ce sera ton tour et que tu verras la grande porte craquer et
remuer, C'est moi de l'autre côté qui suis apres.
    Cf. John XVI, 16: A little while, and now you shall not see me: and
again a little while, and you shall see me. . . .

> You were not promised happiness: work is all
> that is demanded of you.
> Ask the old earth, and it will always answer you
> with bread and wine.[33]

But the Claudelian message of joy is given in the Christmas scene at Chevoche. As the bells are heard ringing during the midnight Mass, Violaine exclaims with the incarnational ecstasy springing from suffering, "O Mara, a little child is born to us!"[34] And as the child of Mara that has been entrusted as a corpse moves on Violaine's bosom, she cries, interpolating the word of the angels in Bethlehem with her own:

> To us, too, a little child is born!
> Behold I give you tidings of great joy.
> Glory be to God!
> Peace to men on earth.[35]

It is the message of joy and peace which is the spirit of Christmas as it is too of the Resurrection—the peace which men attain, as Christ did, only through intense suffering.

In Claudel's drama, the poetry cannot be separated from the dramatic vision. There is, in *L'Annonce*, an integration of musical pattern and dramatic situation, so that the speech of the characters is an inevitable outflow from their spirit, and their spirit in turn is built up by their speech. And because the dramatist envisions the characters as living in an age of Christian faith, his study of the Bible permeates his thoughts and colors his language. The images that come naturally to the minds of the personages in his play are from the Bible and their rhythm is an echo of the biblical language heard the whole year through the Church liturgy.

To the people in Claudel's drama, life is a violent struggle. Because of the intensity with which they lead their lives, the poetry that they speak possesses dramatic inevitability. Now, the musical pattern found in Claudel's poetry has no precedence in French litera-

---

[33] *Ibid.*, p. 213: Cf. Genesis, III, 17: With labour and toil shalt thou eat thereof all the days of thy life.

[34] *Ibid.*, p. 196; cf. Is. IX, 6: For a child is born to us, and a son is given to us. . . .

[35] *Ibid.*, p. 200; cf. Luke II, 14: Glory to God in the highest: and on earth peace to men of good will.

ture. According to the poet himself, the rhythm of his verse is that of a constant rise and fall which we find in nature. Claudel claims that in poetry the movement of the soul is expressed by scales of vibrations noticed in the contraction of the human heart.[36] Inasmuch as emotions cannot all be expressed in regular rhythm, the verse in Claudel's dramas possess that flexibility required to convey the sentiments of the personages.

The rhythm, subordinate though it is to the content of the spoken lines, becomes a unifying element in L'Annonce, integrating the diverse emotions of the characters into a harmonious, artistic presentation of life. The changing rhythms which Claudel creates in this play become, so to speak, an accompaniment to the biblical language which reveals a kaleidoscopic variety of effects evoked to portray the persons with their evolving moods.

Murder in the Cathedral: A Synthesis

From the point of view of language, Murder in the Cathedral possesses something in common with the three preceding verse plays that have been studied. In each of these four plays, the dramatist's vision predominates, animating the action and the dialogue of the play. O'Neill's vision of eternal recurrence hovers through the incantatory lines of Lazarus Laughed; Christopher Fry finds in A Sleep of Prisoners the modern version of the paschal mystery, the passage from suffering to a realization of the nearness of eternity; Claudel builds in L'Annonce Faite à Marie a harmonious world of the supernatural in which woman offers herself as a victim for her family, for her country and for Christendom. And Eliot in Murder in the Cathedral shares his vision of a historical personage reliving Christ's Passion, strengthening the Church by the sacrifice of his life in witness to the law of God above the law of man.

Although in each of these above-mentioned plays the dramatist is engrossed in the presentation of a unique world view with which he is apparently sympathetic, he does not lose sight of the world of the common man who may not quite see eye to eye with the drama-tist. The realistic characters have been provided in each play as a

---

[36] Introduction to Paul Claudel: Oeuvre Poetique, by Stanislas Fumet (Galli-mard, 1957), p. xviii.

countermovement, Caligula and Pompeia in O'Neill's drama, Mara in Claudel's, David King in Christopher Fry's, and the tempters and the knights in Eliot's *Murder in the Cathedral*. The presence of these realistic characters, in the first three plays, however, serves only to make the dramatist's vision clearer. The realistic elements are, so to speak, swallowed up in the grandeur of the view being presented.

The case is different with *Murder in the Cathedral*. The grandeur of the vision of the supernatural world of which Thomas is a part does not diminish the rugged realism of the world of the natural order represented by the tempters and the knights. The clash of the supernatural world with the natural, resulting in the triumph of the former through apparent annihilation, provides a picture in which both worlds come out in striking contrast to form an unmistakable mirror of the society we are acquainted with through history and through contemporary events. In the obvious clash of these two powers, the milieu is influenced now by one, now by the other; but in the end, the witnesses are swayed in the direction of supernatural influence.

If one strives to analyze the elements that contribute to such a moving presentation of the supernatural and the natural orders in society, one inevitably recognizes that a great part is due to Eliot's most skillful handling of language. In presenting the paradox of victory through failure, of rebirth through death, of joy through sorrow, of glory through annihilation, Eliot has achieved an orchestration of varied styles, both of poetry and of prose, which is inimitable in English literature. Eliot himself has called *Murder in the Cathedral* a "dead end" in the sense that "it did not solve the problem of language for future plays."[37] This statement is no disparagement to the dramatist's accomplishment, however, but rather a modest way of saying that a masterpiece is beyond imitation. Genius often expresses itself in the inspiration of creation which happens once for all and allows no repetition. In the world of the artist, the energy that is released in the moment of the creation of a simple masterpiece cannot be summoned at will for another work of the same proportions.

In his Harvard lecture on "Poetry and Drama" quoted above, T.S. Eliot declared that a mixture of prose and verse in the same place is generally to be avoided. According to him, the transition from verse to prose, and vice versa, is only "justifiable when the author

---

37 T.S. Eliot, *Poetry and Drama* (London: Faber & Faber, 1950), p. 23.

wishes to transport the audience violently from one plane of reality to another."[38] This is precisely what Eliot does in *Murder in the Cathedral,* not only in the transitions from verse to prose, and vice versa, but likewise in the passing from one style of verse to another. What Eliot achieved in this drama is a highly complicated musical pattern in which the style is being continually adapted to the speaker's mood, to the atmosphere which the dramatist wishes to create, as well as to the development of thought at the particular point in the drama in which the lines are being spoken.

The parts recited by the chorus of the Canterbury women are most sensitively adapted to their varying moods. The opening lines of the play project the women's presentiment of danger. The feeling of uncertainty and insecurity is expressed by comparatively long complex lines, ending with a three-stress line which makes the transition to other three-stress lines describing their condition during the past seven years, and their wish to be left alone to their accustomed quiet. This is followed once more by irregular lines denoting fear in the disturbance of the quiet seasons, the fear of "winter bringing death from the sea," "Ruinous spring" beating at their doors, "Disastrous summer" burning up the beds of their streams. They fear that their poor will wait only for another "decaying October," and that the summer will bring no consolation for their "autumn fires" and "winter fogs." These images of dreaded misfortune have a cumulative effect which is clinched by two brief lines in which they define their position being "only to wait and to witness."

This movement from complex lines to those with three stresses, and vice versa, is continued in the choral parts, the number of three-stress lines varying every time. Toward the end when the hymn "Dies Irae"[39] is sung in the distance, the recitation of the chorus shows the structural influence of the hymn. The final lines of the play also spoken by the chorus are again affected by the singing of the "Te Deum"[40] in the distance. The complex lines of the ending roll into praise and affirmation of God's ways, the mercies of His continued act of redemption through the blood of His martyrs and saints which enriches the earth. In contrast with these complex lines are the three-

---

[38] *Ibid.,* p. 13.
[39] A hymn sung in the Catholic Mass for the dead.
[40] A hymn of thanksgiving.

stress lines of the traditional prayer of the litany of the saints in which the invocation to Blessed Thomas ends the whole play.

Together with the transitions in style, Eliot makes use of devices, among which is the rhetorical question. At the opening of the play, the series of questions is very expressive of the presentiments the women of Canterbury have:

> Are we drawn by danger? Is it the knowledge of
> safety that draws our feet
> Towards the cathedral? What danger can be
> For us, the poor, the poor women of Canterbury?
> what tribulation
> With which we are not already familiar?

The second part of the play opens with another set of questions maintaining the feeling of anxiety. The questions asked are not merely an ornament, but rather an outlet of the heart that wonders and fears, oppressed by the feeling of uncertainty.

More prevalent is the device of repetition of words and phrases that aid in the building up of atmosphere. The word "danger" is used thrice in the opening lines of Part I, the word "wait," five times. Analysis of the choral parts will show how many words are repeated for cumulative effect. Outstanding among the repetitions is the phrase "Living and partly living" which Eliot obviously wishes to impress on the audience as the psychological condition of the chorus during the Archbishop's seven-year absence.

The choral parts are in themselves a considerable achievement. Chanted by the Canterbury women at seven points, they make the psychological movement of the drama present to the audience. The heavy air of approaching danger and of the weight of seven years' waiting in the opening chorus gives way to the desire that the Archbishop leave them, "the small folk who live among many small things." To them, the coming of the Archbishop is a strain, seeming to draw them into "the pattern of fate." Then the feeling rises in intensity at the end of Part I, with a cumulation of images of foreboding: the owl, the rain, the wind, the flame, the watchman and the mastiff; unhappy experiences are recalled, a past of oppression, torture, extortion, violence, destitution, disease: "The old without fire in winter, the child without milk in summer." (*Collected Plays,* p. 29).

From memories of the past seven years during which they have built "a partial shelter,/For sleeping and eating and drinking and laughter," they turn to the new terror with a sense of being abandoned by God. The ensuing images of "the stifling scent of despair" and "the forms that take shape in the dark air":

> Puss-purr of leopard, footfall of padding bear,
> Palm-pat of nodding ape, square hyaena waiting
> For laughter, laughter, laughter. The Lords of Hell
>   are here.
> They curl round you, lie at your feet, swing and wing
>   through the dark air.

These lines evince the hysterical condition of the women at the approach of the danger they foresee happening in their midst.

Then comes Christmas Day. And the sermon of the Archbishop has a calming effect on the chorus, for Part II commences in a quieter vein. And despite the feeling of uncertainty that still lingers in the lines, there is a recognition that

> The peace of this world is always uncertain, unless
>   men keep the peace of God.
> And war among men defiles this world, but death
>   in the Lord renews it,
> And the world must be cleared in the winter, or we
>   shall have only
> A sour spring, a parched summer, an empty harvest.

The length of the lines aids in creating a certain feeling of serenity that has descended upon the women, making them realize the necessity of the cleansing of the world that must happen in the winter. And with the uncertainty that still remains and the fear of a bitter spring, there is already a note of hope in the line, "The wind stored up in the East." (C.Pl., p. 35).

Previous to the entrance of the knights, seeing the Archbishop determined that "They shall find the shepherd here; the flock shall be spared," the women have attained a realization of the horror of sin aroused by the foreboding of the murder of their spiritual leader. They are now aware that sin is:

> Emptiness, absence, separation from God;
> The horror of the effortless journey, to
>   the empty land
> Which is no land, only emptiness, absence, the Void,
>   the void,
> Where those who were men can no longer turn the mind

> To distraction, delusion, escape into dream, pretence,
> Where the soul is no longer deceived, for there are
> > no objects, no tones.
> No colours, no forms to distract, to divert the soul
> From its seeing itself, foully united forever,
> > nothing with nothing.
> > (C.Pl., p. 44)

Their vision has been, so to speak, corrected. They no longer think only of their quiet living, nor is their only anxiety to keep away from danger. They now consider the meaning of separation from God through sin, and the horror that befalls the man who enters eternity in this state. From this spiritual state they are prepared to feel the intensity of grief upon the murder of the Archbishop (C.Pl., pp. 47–48). It is as if they have part in the guilt, and they cannot cry enough to have the air and the sky clean, the wind and the stones washed. They themselves feel that they have been defiled. And with this awareness, they know that they can no longer look at the day and its common things without seeing them smeared with blood. They consider the petty griefs of life, the personal sorrows as nothing beside the magnitude and depth of this "eternity of evil and wrong" that has defiled them, their houses, their city and the world. This passionate wailing at the death of the Archbishop gives way to a hymn of praise of God even in the martyrdom of Thomas, a hymn that "brings us to a condition of serenity, stillness, and reconciliation," which, according to Eliot, is ultimately the function of art.[41]

The whole gamut of feelings has been aptly expressed by the chorus in *Murder in the Cathedral*, the language of the Canterbury women varying with their moods and sentiments which represent the desired response of the audience to the action in the play.

If the choral parts have the sensitivity of the tides, the words of Thomas are the moon that works on the ebb and flow of emotion in the chorus. The dignity and strength that dominate the lines spoken by Thomas do not allow of as much variation of rhythm as is found in the chorus, but the variation is distinguishable with every change of scene. One feels his understanding compassion for the women who "know and do not know what it is to act or suffer" and who are "fixed in an eternal action" to which they "must consent that it may

---

[41] Cf. Carol H. Smith, *T.S. Eliot's Dramatic Theory and Practice* (Princeton: Princeton University Press, 1963), p. 30.

be willed." He knows that despite their fear of suffering, this is part of God's design for them. This awareness of a truth which is beyond the realization of the women at the opening of the play is expressed in a pattern of iambic pentameter lines in which there is a tone of stability.

When speaking to the priests, the Archbishop narrates the events preceding his arrival at Canterbury in tetrameter lines, the quicker movement betraying the tenseness of the situation of pursuit by the enemies. This verse prepares the audience for the "more subtle, and sometimes rather crabbed...four-stress rhyming verse for the Tempters who dramatize the tortuous progress of Becket's inner struggle."[42] With these Tempters, Thomas speaks in wary, four-stress verses that possess the weight of thought and the determination to act according to principles. The sharpness of his questions and the firmness of his replies present a striking contrast with the beguiling tone of the Tempters.

One of the most outstanding variations in the verse style can be noticed in the taunting jazz rhythm of the Knights, with its cheap-sounding rhyme describing Thomas as

> the tradesman's son:
> the backstairs brat who was born in Cheapside;
> There is the creature that crawled upon the king;
> swollen with blood and swollen with pride.
> Creeping out of the London dirt,
> Crawling up like a louse on your shirt,
> The man who cheated, swindled, lied; broke his oath
> and betrayed his King. (C.Pl., p. 38)

Toward the end of the play, swinging in a still more jazz-like rhythm are the quatrains spoken by the Knights, who, drunken, come in to assault the Archbishop. As Carol Smith has pointed out, these lines resemble Vachel Lindsay's "Daniel Jazz."[43]

> Where is Becket, the traitor to the King?
> Where is Becket, the meddling priest?
> Come down Daniel to the Lions' den,
> Come down Daniel for the mark of the beast.
>
> Are you washed in the blood of the Lamb?
> Are you marked with the mark of the beast?

---

42 E. Martin Browne, quoted in Carol H. Smith, *ibid.,* p. 102.
43 *Ibid.,* p. 100.

> Come down Daniel to the lions' den,
> Come down Daniel and join in the feast.
>
> Where is Becket the Cheapside brat?
> Where is Becket the faithless priest?
> Come down Daniel to the lions' den.
> Come down Daniel and join in the feast.
>   (C.Pl., p. 46)

The answers of Thomas while now and then parodying their style through easy rhyming, maintain the strength of wit, logic and sincerity.

Most fully savoring of Thomas' character, however, are his words at the end of Part I summing up his life history, and the sermon he delivers on Christmas morning mirroring his own thoughts on the reconciliation of opposites in the Church: the birth and the death of Christ celebrated at one and the same time in the Holy Mass said on the feast of His Nativity; the peace of Christ which is not the peace that the world gives; the simultaneous mourning and rejoicing over the death of the martyr; the elevation of the Saints in Heaven because they had made themselves most low on earth.

It is especially the contrast in the style of the sermon in prose and the Knights' speeches spoken after the murder of Thomas that reveal most fully Eliot's power in the manipulation of language. To analyze both is to notice the elevated tone in the simple sincerity of the Archbishop's sermon on the one hand, and the emptiness and unconvincing veneer of the Knights' speeches on the other, condemning themselves by their very arguments in their defense. There is a rhythm in the Archbishop's sermon—the harmonious movement of the mind and heart ready to go to God. In the Knights' speeches, there is a looseness of utterance, a slackness that gives the impression of words which, though piled up, do not adhere together, symbolizing the disintegration of spirit experienced by the speakers. The jolt produced by the vast difference in these prose styles as well as by the transitions in verse styles is symbolical of the gap between the world of the supernatural order and that of the natural order, so that the supernatural produces an impact on the natural which comes as a shock to the audience.

The preceding discussion of *Murder in the Cathedral* has shown that it combines the language of the dramas previously considered, having both the quality of the play presenting a dramatist's vision, and that of the play that is desirous of involving the audience in the

problem perceived by the dramatist, thus making use of argumentative
devices. The incantatory language of O'Neill's *Lazarus Laughed* is
here, even surpassing this language in the variety of devices used.
The archetypal utterance of Fry's *A Sleep of Prisoners* is here, not
distributed to various characters, but concentrated in the figure of
Thomas as the archetype of Christ and the martyrs. But along with
highly inspired lines, one listens to the jazz rhythms of the Knights
and to their language that borrows from the terminology of modern
parliamentary procedure in the effort to justify their repulsive deed.
This spirit of parody brings us back to the *J. B.* of MacLeish, to the
Back to Methuselah of Shaw, and the *Judith* of Giraudoux. The effect
of the combination of styles in *Murder in the Cathedral* is the impression of a subtly orchestrated piece.

* * *

From this study of the language used for biblical themes in a
number of modern plays, some points stand out conspicuously.
The dramatist is seen to use argumentative language—discussion or
debate—first, when he holds an interpretation of a biblical theme
different from that which has been approved by Christian exegetes,
or when it is not clear which view is tenable; secondly, when the
dramatist is strongly aware of the divided view of his audience regarding the interpretation of the biblical theme. Hence, language that is
argumentative in nature would be fitted to the epic theatre which has
as one of its aims, to stimulate thought along new channels rather than
to uphold the traditional. This is clearly the case with *J. B.*

The incantatory style of poetry, the style that strives in the building up of atmosphere like the symbolists', the archetypal utterance,
the expression of the collective unconscious, are adapted to the dramas
in which the playwright attempts to share a vision with his audience.
Being so taken up by his vision, the dramatist tries to transport his
audience by the magic of his language. Hence, the language most
appropriate for this kind of drama is inspired poetry which possesses
sufficient pliability for expressing varying moods.

Combining language with the qualities of a vision and language
that retains relevance to the modern situation, Eliot has written
Murder in the Cathedral in a language that is a synthesis of disparate
elements of structure and tonal effects.

CHAPTER FIVE

The Problem of Classification

COMEDY WITH BIBLICAL DIMENSION

Solemnity might naturally be expected as the atmosphere of a play with a biblical theme. The history of mystery plays in England, however, demonstrates that the comic spirit has not been considered incompatible with the presentation of biblical themes. There is the famous scene of Noah's wife, for instance, who draws the laughter of the audience by her shrewish ways. In Shakespeare's comedy, the expression "a merry devil" is a reminder of the horse play that actors could indulge in when acting the part of the under-devils in certain scenes of mystery and miracle plays.

In our own times, neither is the comic spirit absent from plays with a biblical theme. Among the plays considered in this study, at least two can be classified as comedies: *A Sleep of Prisoners* and *Cantique de Cantiques.*

Comedy has from early times been regarded as a copy of life, a mirror of custom, a reflection of truth intended to correct foibles and ridicule disagreeable habits.[1] In his essay entitled "Comedy,"[2] Fry has thrown new light on the subject. To him, comedy is "an escape, not from truth but from despair: a narrow escape into faith." And the faith that he believes comedy to possess is that trust in "a universal cause for delight." He thinks that comedy has a special worth in our times "when the loudest faith has been faith in a trampling materialism,

---

[1] Cf. Carlo Goldini, "The Comic Theatre," in *European Theories of the Drama* by Barrett H. Clark, p. 200, and George Meredith, "An Essay" on Comedy," p. 439 of the same volume.

[2] In *Adelphi* xxvii, 27 (November 1950); also reprinted in *The Tulane Drama Review,* iv, 3 (March 1960).

when literature has been thought unrealistic which did not mark and
remark our poverty and doom." It is Fry's intention that comedy
should redeem joy from its low companions such as the mockery and
ridicule which have been found so often in comic plays. The dramatist
claims that through and in comedy, we come to discover the meaning
of life: for, "groaning as we may be, we move in the figure of a dance,
and so moving we trace the outline of the mystery." It was probably
from this statement that Spanos took the hint for the title of his essay,
" 'A Sleep of Prisoners': The Choreography of Comedy." [3]

Judging by the episodes Fry chooses from Holy Scripture, one
may say that his intention is to illuminate the meaning of the prisoners'
night as well as the significance of war. The Cain-Abel conflict apparently points to jealousy as the age-old cause which in modern terms
is the rivalry among the nations often leading to war. The rebellion
of Absalom against King David could be interpreted as war that,
in the sequence of events, is the punishment for the excesses of
rulers, a condition which, even in our days, is a conceivable cause of
war. In the case of the Abraham-Isaac episode, however, the human
sacrifice is demanded by God as a test of faith: this holds true in the
case of well-meaning nations and peoples to whom the sacrifice of their
soldiers is a racking trial which they endure in their adherence to the
cause of right. The predicament of the three young men in the furnace
suggests the desperate situation of soldiers and their miraculous safety
from the danger that has seemed so all-enclosing as to be inescapable.
The more we consider Fry's intention in depicting war, the more
we are tempted to think that his material would be more fittingly
presented in tragedy rather than in comedy. Yet, *A Sleep of Prisoners*
has been classified as comedy.[4] To find an explanation of the anomaly,
we need to refer to Fry's own essay on comedy quoted earlier in this
section. Recalling an episode that helped him to form his idea of
comedy, Fry writes:

> A friend once told me that when he was under influence of ether
> he dreamed he was turning over the pages of a great book, in which he
> knew he would find, on the last page, the meaning of life. The pages of
> the book were alternately tragic and comic, and he turned page after page,
> his excitement growing, not only because he was approaching the answer

---

[3] See note 34, Chapter II.
[4] Cf. Spanos, *ibid.*

but because he couldn't know, until he arrived, on which side of the book the final page would be. At last it came: the universe opened up to him in a hundred words: and they were uproariously funny. He came back to consciousness crying with laughter, remembering everything. He opened his lips to speak. It was then that the great and comic answer plunged back out of his reach.

If I had to draw a picture of the person of Comedy it is so I should like to draw it: the tears of laughter running down the face, one hand still lying on the tragic page which so nearly contained the answer, the lips about to frame the great revelation, only to find it had gone as disconcertingly as a chair twitched away when we went to sit down.[5]

Now, in *A Sleep of Prisoners,* when we come to the last pages, it does seem as though the meaning of the life of suffering in war has suddenly opened up to us. Yet, we cannot say that it looks "uproariously funny." The phrase does not, of course, belong to Christopher Fry, but to his friend. In Fry's own words, "Comedy has tears of laughter running down the face, one hand still lying on the tragic page which so nearly contained the answer, the lips about to frame the great revelation, only to find it had gone as disconcertingly as a chair twitched away when we went to sit down." To Fry, the tragic and the comic are found together in the same play. The effect of the discovery of the great and comic answer, therefore, need not be uproarious laughter. It could rather be that sensation described by Fry's friend, Charles Williams, when he said, "When we're dead we shall have the sensation of having enjoyed life altogether, whatever has happened to us."[6] To have "enjoyed life altogether" does not necessarily imply thinking of it as uproariously funny. Meredith wrote to the point when he said,

> The laughter of comedy is impersonal and of unrivaled politeness, nearer a smile—often no more than a smile. It laughs through the mind, for the mind directs it; and it might be called the humor of the mind.
>
> One excellent test of the civilization of a country, as I have said, I take to be the flourishing of the comic idea and comedy: and the test of true comedy is that it shall awaken thoughtful laughter.[7]

A Sleep of Prisoners evokes this smile that Meredith speaks of—a thoughtful laughter which is aroused by the sight of prisoners trying

---

5 Christopher Fry; see note 2 above.
6 *Ibid.*
7 George Meredith, *loc. cit.*

to accommodate themselves to the inconveniences of prison life, more irritable than ordinary people because of the tensions they experience, so much so, that the impressions they get in their waking hours find expression in their dreams. We laugh at their oddness, the endless quaintness of their spirit, but the laughter is not all. We think of the implications of the single night experienced by the prisoners with their tensions and their dreams. And seeing them becoming more understanding of their situation and more tolerant of one another, we feel, if not the gloriously joyous ending of Shakespeare's great comedies, at least the acceptance of life and the feeling of hope with which modern comedies, like *The Cocktail Party,* end.

In *A Sleep of Prisoners* we are reminded of Fry's own statement that when he set about writing a comedy, the idea presented itself first of all as tragedy.[8] "A bridge has to be crossed, a thought has to be turned. Somehow the characters have to unmortify themselves: to affirm life and assimilate death and persevere in joy." This we find the characters doing in *A Sleep of Prisoners.* They are learning to find that the state they are in is far from perfect.

> In a sort of a universe and a bit of a fix:
> It's what they call flesh we're in.
> And a fine old dance it is.

Thus, they accept their situation with its discomforts. "Well, sleep, I suppose," says Adams at the end. And even the unruly David adds a blessing, "Yeh, God bless!" It is Peter who wishes joy in the tradition of Christmas, "Rest you merry." Meadows ends the play with the words, "Hope so. Hope so," which we may consider to be the English paraphrase for the Latin "Amen."

The experience of the four prisoners during a single night has indeed been shown as the distillation of dark into light, which, according to Fry, is the natural process of comedy. If the play ends as it does, it is only because the prisoners trust that despite their temporary discomforts, there is "universal cause for delight."

Closer to the traditional notion of comedy as a copy of life so unexpectedly true as to evoke laughter, is Giraudoux's *Cantique de Cantiques,* the one-act play with a minimum of biblical theme. Unlike

---

8 Christopher Fry, *ibid.*
See also Adolf D. Karmann, "Friedrich Duerrenmatt and the Tragic Sense of Comedy," in *The Tulane Drama Review* iv, 4 (May 1960), 77.

A Sleep of Prisoners, which is heavy with meaning, Giraudoux's piece aims at delighting the audience rather than posing some weighty truth. The comic spirit pervades the play, in its character presentation, the quaintness of the phrase it employs, and above all, in the unexpected turn of events which takes one's breath with laughter.

M. le President, doubtless beyond his fifties, and baldheaded, if we may take the cashier's hint, is still searching for romance with "the most charming of young ladies," on the terrace of some French café overlooking some beautiful landscape. He likes to talk, almost as in a monologue, about things he imagines. Speaking of the visitors at the café, he says:

> . . . Yes, they come, Victor! And at last they achieve their minute of happiness, of peace, of interlude before they go back to their various duties—their careers, their homes, perhaps the cares of the nation. Yet Gods knows you serve them badly. You wipe your foreheads with the napkin you have for wiping the glasses. Coffee is always slopped into the saucer. Cups of chocolate swim with tea-leaves. You give the chessboard to those who want to play bridge, the draughtsboard arrives when one wants a game of belote. And yet they love you. All the reserve of good humor cunningly stolen from their families, all the inner kindliness which they have managed to preserve after all the world's crises and disasters—they keep all of this for this meeting with you, a meeting as speechless but as passionate as that of Tristan and Yseult—(turning to the cashier) am I not right?—in which their only words are your Christian names and the name of whatever potion you give them to drink.[9]

The Cashier has to correct him, "Not everything you say is quite accurate, sir." Evidently, M. le President thinks eloquence his strong point, but his efforts are at best exhibited as grandiloquence, and at times end in transparent banality, as when he praises Victor for his name: "It's a good name," he says. "It means victorious"—as if his comment added anything new. Despite his experience and his power, he is outwitted by all the personnel of the café.

Florence is of course the central figure in the play, for the greater part of the lines make up her song—she calls it a dirge—of complaint about her young man, alternating with praises of her elderly M. le President. The outpouring of her grievances becomes rather impressive. Describing Jerome as the god of little accidents, she says:

---

9 Giraudoux, "The Song of Songs," tr. John Raikes, *The Tulane Drama Review*, III, 4 (May 1959), 89.

If there's anything hot about, he'll burn himself on it. If there's anything to stumble over, he'll stumble and hurt himself. In every doorway he pinches his fingers. Whenever there's an umbrella open, the points stick into his eyes. In the last month I've got to know every variety of massage and dressing and embrocation. In the middle of the night warts grow on his fingers. I spend my life anointing him, mending the holes he's made in himself. What with splinters, with nails on his car, I have to suck his blood ten times a day. If a serpent had been given the special mission of biting him endlessly, I should have no more to do than I have. He's the god of little accidents.[10]

Moreover, comparing Jerome to M. le President, she adds, "He may be handsome. But he isn't nice."[11] To Florence, Jerome's childishness is boring:

With you I was only aware of great professions and great undertakings. I used to know about and follow world struggles, world needs, world treasures. With you it was oil, gold, iron. With him it's celluloid, chromium plate, tin, aluminum. He has a pocket workshop. He knows all about mending watch-chains, all the alloys used for clasps. He's the god of little metals.[12]

Then she proceeds to the praises of M. le President, so that one would think she would finally return to him. Her next unexpected announcement takes one all the more by surprise: "This is why I came, Claude. I'm getting married. . . . I'm going to marry this young man, Jerome."[13] And what she adds is still more surprising after all that she has confessed about her young man: "We understand each other. We like each other. We shall be happy." This inconsistency can be explained only by her own words,

I was suddenly seized with a desire to complain, to air my grievances. It was just like an urge to stretch, to shout, to sing. Yes, that's what it was—the need to sing. I had a theme in my head, a pathetic theme. I tried it out in all its possible forms, I treated it like a fugue. It was my fugue with you. But it's of no importance, and it had no sense, either.[14]

---

10 *Ibid.,* p. 94.
11 *Ibid.,* p. 95.
12 *Ibid.,* p. 96.
13 *Ibid.,* p. 98.
14 *Ibid.*

As for Jerome, he is all that Florence speaks about him—an innocence beyond suspicion and jealousy. His appearance is one of the most unexpected episodes of the play—Florence's fiancé coming up to her former lover, introducing himself to him, and taking him aback by unexpected praises. In Jerome's disarming innocence, his very weakness is the power which vanquishes M. le President. In presenting Jerome, Giraudoux makes full use of the effect of connivance. A little before his return, Florence had been telling M. le President that Jerome's invariable question was, "Are you ready?" She had confided then that some day she would have to ask him, "Ready for what?" Now when Jerome had returned to fetch her, his question naturally popped up, "Well, are you ready, Florence?" With a note of daring she answered, "For what, Jerome?" But when he repeated, "I asked you if you were ready," her reply inevitably came, "Yes, I'm ready." There is another instance of the strong contrast between Jerome's innocence and the lover-like connivance of M. le President and Florence. After returning to M. le President the jewels she had received from him on various occasions, he once more succeeded to make her receive them anew one by one. At the end she places them all in a bag as a secret, M. le President had suggested, with which to protect herself against Jerome. And then Jerome comes in all the bliss of one who thinks he is offering something precious for Florence on her birthday. "It's a jacinth. Not a very big one. In fact it's minute. But as it's only paste, it doesn't matter. In fact it's all the better." Trying to cover up the bathetic effect of Florence's receiving paste jacinth after all the precious pearls, emeralds and sapphires, M. le President comments, "It's the intention that matters." Unabashed, Jerome rejoins, "Intention is the word. A true intention with a false jacinth."

Among the café personnel, Victor and the Cashier come out with no little distinction. They prove themselves trained in repartee. Early in the play, M. le President is not too much satisfied with Victor, so he starts talking to him.

> But listen, my friend, are all you waiters as narrow-minded as that?...
> No! You won't shut me up. I'm well-known to be the most obstinate
> orator in Europe!... must you all go on misunderstanding what your
> customers are to you and you to them? Will your union realize in the
> end that the finest café—yours if you like—is in the last resort no more
> than a meeting place—let me speak!—a meeting-place between the waiter

and the customer? What do you think customers look for in a café?
It isn't your coffee, which is always filthy—I insist upon silence!—it's
you... The sight of their regular waiter—yet God knows you're not
handsome.[15]

When he is at last able to interrupt M. le President's eloquence,
Victor says,

> My dear sir, there must be a misunderstanding then. Speaking for us,
> the waiters, I can only say that we do not love our customers—I mean
> our regular customers—we adore them! How else do you think we manage
> to stick it all our lives giving out drinks when we're not thirsty and
> sandwiches when we're not hungry? We have as many talents as the rest
> of you, sir. There's a waiters' academy. Some of us have degrees. I should
> have made an excellent life-saver. I can't swim, but in life-saving it's cool-
> ness which counts, not swimming. No, instead of painting or life-saving
> we stay down among the crowd, the screaming, swearing, sweating crowd,
> because we know we shall see, each in its turn, at its proper time and in its
> proper place, seeming to come out of the walls, the faces of our regular
> customers. . . .[16]

And the Cashier knowingly remarks: "They aren't always so handsome,
either, M. le President, sir. . ."

Volubly speaking for the waiters, Victor assures him that they
love their customers: "They revive the taste in all concoctions so stale
for us. *They* are our refreshing draught at dawn, our midday brandy,
our cooling drink at evening. When we meet, our exchange is only
little words, looks, smiles, but we love them, M. le President, we love
them, and a café without regular customers—the cashier will confirm
this—is like a church without chapels."[17]

The Cashier corrects him: "Without saints, he means. His simile
is less exact than yours, sir."

The most uproarious fun resulting from their connivance, however, issues from their suggesting Table Number Two to be used by
the romantic M. le President and his most charming of young ladies
as the most conducive to feminine gentleness. In the middle of their
conversation, Florence asks, "Are you sure no one is listening?" And
the Cashier assures them, "No, no one." When Jerome had left with

15 *Ibid.*, p. 88.
16 *Ibid.*, p. 89.
17 *Ibid.*, p. 90.

his Florence, however, Victor remarked, "If I were you, I'd have a try, M. le President."

"A try at what, Victor?" asks the President.

"To get her back from Jerome. It's not impossible," replies Victor.

"Ah! so you heard," asks M. le President in consternation. And Victor explains: "Everyone heard. I forgot to tell you Table Two is like a sounding board. It corresponds acoustically to Number Eleven on the other side. You could have put Mlle. Florence at Number Eleven, and she wouldn't have missed a word." But even this report fails to excite M. le President. He is an entirely beaten man.

And the play might have become tragic were it not for the fact that it has caused too many laughs so far. To avoid giving M. le President the air of a crestfallen man, Giraudoux sends someone to look for him at the end of the play. "It's the Prime Minister's chauffeur looking for you, M. le President," the Page announces.

"Ah, it's you, Laurence? What have you come for?" he asks, not a little relieved.

And the chauffeur assures him, "For you, M. le President. The Prime Minister told me to find you wherever you might be, and to bring you back. As fast as I could make the car move. He said laughingly that it was a matter of saving the Republic."

The President answers: "He has come in the nick of time. I will come at once." The nick of time for M. le President was the moment when he did not know what to do with himself. It was extremely good for his self-respect there and then that he should feel he was being wanted for "a matter of saving the Republic."

Although the play gives us no really "great revelation," it is indeed, as Fry has claimed, "an escape from despair"—the despair caused by the complexity in a woman's changing psychology. It is a saving escape delightfully effected through the realization of the truth of everyday life, that a woman's complaints are often merely a refrain in a song which, according to Giraudoux, is more of a physical compulsion than the expression of spiritual states.

A second realization arrived at in the play is that the younger lover is often the stronger, no matter how affluent, how generous and how powerful the elder one may be. It is in this point that the playwright claims the right to use the title "Song of Songs." The truth he is dealing with is a long-standing one. It was already felt and expressed in ages long past, in the time of the great lover—King Solomon himself. For the young woman whom the king would have wanted to be his bride was longing for her younger lover, despite all the comfort and wealth that the king could offer her.

The comedy of *Cantique de Cantiques*, however, does not depend on a scrupulous presentation of the biblical theme for its effect. Giraudoux is merely suggesting that the incomprehensible and highly amusing intricacies of a woman's psychology in a love triangle is but a renewal of its archetype found in biblical poetry. In making us aware of this, Giraudoux exhibits once more his aptitude for the witty phrase, the presentation of the amusing character and unexpected turn of events which make for sparkling comedy.

On a level quite different from *A Sleep of Prisoners*, Giraudoux's comedy ends with an acceptance of life with its eccentricities. The escape from despair is not into faith, as Fry thinks it is, but it is nonetheless an affirmation of our "position in time."[18]

BIBLICAL TRAGEDY

In I. A. Richards' well-known statement, "The least touch of any theology which has a compensating Heaven to offer the tragic hero is fatal,"[19] he has kindled one of the major discussions in the study of drama in recent times. To him, "Tragedy is only possible to a mind which is for the moment agnostic or Manichean."[20] Laurence Michel supports this contention in proposing the thesis that nothing in literature has yet come forth which is both Christian and tragic at the same time: "Christianity is intransigent to tragedy: tragedy bucks and balks under Christianity."[21] The Judeao-Christian culture having a common source, and the Bible being the treasury for this culture, to deny the possibility of a Christian tragedy would be equivalent to saying the same thing of biblical tragedy.

Richards' statement implies a concept of tragedy which makes a certain sense of utter helplessness, a despair unrelieved by hope of a

---

[18] Christopher Fry, *op. cit.*, p. 78.
[19] *Principles of Literary Criticism* (New York: Harcourt, Brace, 1948), p. 246.
[20] *Ibid.*
[21] *Thought* (Autumn, 1956), 427. Quoted by P. Milward in *Shakespeare Studies*, I (1962), 13.

heaven, essential. It is in line with a modern view that the " 'tragic' must contain also a cosmic sense of the problem of evil, the mystery of the cruelty of things."[22] With this view of tragedy, I would like to differ. For, although in Greek tragedy we can find this cruelty of fate as in *Oedipus Rex*, we also notice the concept of redemptive suffering as in *Oedipus Coloneus*. I agree with Cleanth Brooks and with Louis Martz that what is essential to tragedy is its presentation of suffering and its affirmation ensuing from the recognition of a secret cause. Theology does not lessen the suffering but makes the reasons for its acceptance clearer and more forcible. The light cast by the Resurrection of Christ does not lessen the darkness that envelops the agony of His crucifixion but rather gives meaning to His anguish. In the words of John Gribben,

> We cannot remove the tragic element from saints or martyrs because we know that their deaths crowned their living. It must be considered that they were flesh and blood, not plaster of Paris (sic) and that their deaths were a dying and not an anesthetized transformation from this world to the next.[23]

Furthermore, I agree with Balthasar that post-Christian tragedy on the stage can be transparent for the tragedy of the Cross.[24] Biblical material is fit for tragic treatment by the very fact that the biblical narrative has for its center the tragedy of the Cross.

Now, we distinguish two aspects to the tragic as presented in the Bible: there is the suffering of Christ, the innocent victim who is betrayed, and whose suffering is an immolation for the redemption of men; and there is the misery of the friend of Christ who turns traitor, failing to respond to his Master's love. A study of biblical characters will show, from Cain and Abel to Judas and Paul, the transparency of these two aspects in the tragedy of the Cross. But whether the emphasis is on the tragedy of love that is betrayed in spite of all its efforts to give itself to the loved one, or the tragedy of the sinner that throws away his chances to make good, spurns love and makes of his life a failure, there remains the liturgical act in the recognition of

---

22 F.L. Lucas, *Tragedy: Serious Drama in Relation to Aristotle's "Poetics"* (Collier Books, 1962), p. 26.

23 "Shaw's 'Saint Joan: a Tragic Heroine," *Thoughts* (Winter, 1965), 551.

24 Hans Urs von Balthasar, "The Tragic and the Christian Faith," *Hochland*, LVII (August 1965), 497-510.

man's limitations in the presence of the Infinite. And this very recognition is the basis for the acceptance of suffering, an acceptance which raises the human sufferer to the sphere of the divine.

Since the time Aristotle gave us his famous definition, no term has been as much studied and discussed in the field of drama as tragedy. So highly have the Greek philosopher's ideas been respected through the centuries that dramatists seemed to be preoccupied in fitting their creation to some sort of Procrustean bed. Even in our own age, which is characterized by experimentation, Aristotle's ideas have not been wholly set aside: He is continually being referred to by students of dramatic literature.

In order to study further the possibility of biblical tragedy, it will be necessary to consider the age-old question "What is tragedy?" In the consideration of this problem, it will be convenient to start with Aristotle.

In the *Poetics*, tragedy is defined as "a representation of an action, which is serious, complete in itself, and of a certain length; it is expressed in speech made beautiful in different ways in different parts of the play; it is acted, not narrated; and by exciting pity and fear, it gives a healthy relief to such emotions."[25] A study of the definition will show that each part of it is worth a lengthy discussion: on the subject matter of tragedy, on the form it employs, on the manner in which it is communicated, and on the function it fulfills.[26] A consideration of opinions held by present-day critics leads us to the conclusion that the key point in the discussion of tragedy is found at the beginning of Aristotle's definition: Tragedy is a representation of an action that is serious. In tragedy, the action presented must be serious, and, if we may judge by the ensuing parts of the definition, its treatment must also be serious, for Aristotle demands that the representation be expressed in "speech made beautiful," and the desired result of the performance is the exciting and purging of the feeling of pity and fear in the spectators.

It is interesting to consider the variations given to Aristotle's definition by modern scholars, who, like the Greek philosopher, have reached their conclusions after a study of masterpieces in the field of

---

25 Lucas, *op. cit.*, p. 25.
26 *Ibid.*

drama. A study of Greek tragedy led Leo Aylen to make the following statement:

> We could say of every extant Greek tragedy that it was a lively meditation, conducted in public, into some issue of permanent significance, using song and dance and verse dialogue to represent an event in ancient history which embodied the particular issue, so that the audience's understanding of the issue should be deepened. This is the common ground of tragedy.[27]

To Aylen, "an action that is serious" means "some issue of permanent significance" embodied in "an event in ancient history." Cleanth Brooks, on the other hand, in a consideration of dramatic literature through the ages, has this to say:

> Tragedy deals with ultimates. . . .
> Under the circumstances, it is a temptation to say that all these "tragedies" treat seriously a life-and-death problem, that this is a sufficient definition to cover all our cases, and that it is perhaps the only definition wide enough to do so. But one can actually be more precise than that: all of these works deal with the meaning of suffering, and in none of them does the hero merely passively endure. . . . On the tragic hero, suffering is never merely imposed: he incurs it by his own decision, or, at the least, he finally wills to accept it as properly pertaining to the nature of things including his own deepest nature.[28]

Aylen's "issue of permanent significance" becomes for Cleanth Brooks "a life-and-death problem" involving suffering which is incurred by the hero, or at least accepted. Two points can be distinguished in the above concept of tragedy: suffering as action, and the acceptance of suffering. Now, this acceptance, according to the same author,

> springs from a desire for knowledge, for the deepest kind of self-knowledge, knowledge of the full meaning of one's ultimate commitment.[29]

Strikingly similar in essence is the statement made by Louis Martz in his study of *The Saint as Tragic Hero:*

---

27 *Greek Tragedy and the Modern World* (London: Methuen and Co., 1964), p. 148.
28 In the Introduction to *Tragic Themes in Western Literature* (New Haven: Yale University Press, c. 1955), pp. 4-5.
29 *Ibid.*

Tragedy, then, seems to demand both the human sufferer and the secret cause: that is to say, the doubt, the pain, the pity of the human sufferer; and the affirmation, the awe, the terror of the secret cause. It is an affirmation even though the cause is destructive in its immediate effects: for this cause seems to affirm the existence of some universal order of things.[30]

It will be noticed that in Martz' statement, there are two elements to be found in the subject matter of tragedy, in consonance both with Aristotle and with Cleanth Brooks, the first element being suffering which arouses in us pity for the human sufferer, and the second, an affirmation of the "existence of some universal order of things," an affirmation which is accompanied by the feeling of "terror of the secret cause" of the suffering.

Hans Urs von Balthasar goes still deeper into the subject in his essay, "Das Tragische und der Christliche Glaube."[31] He makes the statement that the basis of Greek tragedy is myth. To him, however, myth does not mean an invented story, nor yet, as Aylen claims, "stories of ancient history...quite certainly believed in as literally true."[32] The essential point about the Greek myths, according to Balthasar, is that they present a sphere in which human existence is distinguished from that of the gods. In the Greek myths, the divinities normally move in the "sphere beyond," just as men move in the "sphere below." But man with the limitations of his precarious existence possesses a beauty, and attains a sublimity from the fact that he rises into the sphere of the divine light. This full significance of finite existence rising into and coming in touch with divine life is, to Balthasar, the basis of Greek tragedy.[33]

The relationship between the finite and the infinite becomes the basis or cause for the tragic in Greek drama, for in its contact with the divine, man is confronted by mystery. The paradoxes of human existence lead to an endless questioning. In a tragedy, therefore, men "know and do not know,"[34] they suffer the agony of uncertainty. But at the bottom of the paradox of life we find a guilt which defies

---

30 *Ibid.*, p. 153.
31 *Hochland, loc. cit.*
32 *Op. cit.*, p. 148.
33 *Op. cit.*
34 T.S. Eliot, *Murder in the Cathedral* (London: Faber and Faber, 1953), p. 21.

analysis; man is guilty and yet not wholly responsible for the guilt, for the situation often goes beyond his control. In its revelation of the human situation with all its mystery and pain, tragedy presents, in a sense, a liturgical act by which man with all his limitations stands exposed to the gaze of the divine. Balthasar goes on to say that this exposure of the powerlessness of man in many Greek tragedies often borders on rebellion: the rebellion of the Titans against the gods, rebellion against death, sickness and impotence, rebellion against the paradoxical, meaningless, illogical edicts of the gods. But in spite of all the reasons for resistance, the Greek heart shows a still greater force of acceptance when it has looked at things in the light of truth.

Thus, we may reduce Balthasar's concept of the essence of tragedy to the two points previously noticed in Cleanth Brooks and Louis Martz. Tragedy is the presentation of (1) human suffering ensuing from the mystery of finite existence rising into the divine; (2) the acceptance or affirmation of man's terrible existence viewed in the divine light, an acceptance which thus becomes a liturgical act. This is, so to speak, some modern dramatists' version of Aristotle's age-old statement that tragedy is "a representation of an action which is serious." Just what is meant by an action that is serious has been variously elucidated. The action in tragedy is thus an embodiment of human suffering in one form or other, along with the affirmation of the human lot, in degrees ranging from rebellious recognition of some truth of the universal order, to the sublime acceptance by the strong heart that rises to the sphere of the gods.

If the essential element of tragedy is the presentation of action that is serious—that is, of men's suffering that arouses pity, and the acceptance of this suffering consequent to recognition of a secret cause that arouses a feeling akin to terror—the two plays studied in this volume as showing distinct trends in modern dramaturgy must be classified as tragedies. Both plays present characters whose suffering is undeserved. J. B. and Violaine should therefore be analogues of Christ the Innocent One, immolated in an act of worship for the Father, in place of a sinning humanity. In their suffering, both J. B. and Violaine arouse our pity. The end in tragedy, however, should show an affirmation of human suffering, an affirmation resulting from a forceful recognition of a secret cause, whether it be an offense that draws down punishment or a cooperation in the divine plan of redemption. The recognition of the secret cause inherent in the limitations of men and the omnipotence of God excites in us an awe for His power, a fear for the very precariousness of human existence.

Up to the tenth scene in *J. B.*, the hero has been presented as an analogue of Christ whose agony is undeserved. The last (eleventh) scene, however, presents an acceptance of suffering, but it is an acceptance which is not based on a recognition of its secret cause. Until the end, J. B. does not realize the reason for his suffering, but he accepts it simply because he knows the means of bearing it, which is human love. Thus, though *J. B.* has the rudiments of tragedy—the presentation of suffering and its acceptance—it fails to reach the sublimity that should belong to tragedy, which, as Balthasar has put it,[35] shows man rising to the sphere of the divine by the recognition of his limitations in the presence of the infinite, a recognition which constitutes a liturgical act. J. B. is shown as trying to rise to the divine, only to come back in the end, to the human sphere, without having recognized the meaning of providential design.

In *L'Annonce faite à Marie,* the transparency for the tragedy of the Cross is strikingly evident. A double aspect of this biblical tragedy is present in the play: the tragedy of Violaine who, like Christ, immolates herself for others, only to be betrayed; and the tragedy of the sister and fiancé who betray her into suffering, both on account of their inability to comprehend her and on account of the very baseness of their nature, thus calling down misery on themselves.

The affirmation of suffering at the end of the play is the result of a powerfully convincing recognition of the secret cause of Violaine's suffering in the Communion of Saints by which she is rendered victim for the Church, for her country and for her family, whereas those who had betrayed her, Mara and Jacques, recognize the cause of their suffering and Violaine's in their own mistaken follies. The effect of this recognition on the spectator is not merely pity, intense compassion for the sufferers, but also an awe in the contemplation of the events that constitute the divine plan, a fear which is the beginning of wisdom.

According to Aristotle, the most important element of tragedy is plot. This statement has been much challenged by modern drama.

---

[35] *Op. cit.*

Opposed to the classical sense of plot in which events are causally connected, Brecht has proposed the epic theatre in which action may be episodic. Rather than action, Maeterlinck has emphasized feeling— an awareness of the invisible in his static drama.

Now, a study of events presented in the Bible will reveal that there is in them an episodic quality. For the biblical method of presentation is that of parataxis. What is emphasized in the biblical account is not the subordination of one event to another by the establishment of their causal relationship, but rather the treatment of each event in its relation to the divine plan. The Greek method, to employ Auerbach's term, may be considered "hypotactical," each event being subordinated to another by the relationship of cause and effect.

The action in *J. B.* is characterized by the biblical parataxis, each event being an episode whose meaning lies in its direct relationship with God. This reflection of the biblical method might be responsible for the solemnity which pervades the scenes presenting the misfortunes befalling J. B. For, upon hearing the announcement of each event, J. B. addresses himself to God, who, he believes, has permitted the occurrence. Together with J. B., the audience want to know God's answer to his question on the reason for human suffering. And it is this attentive waiting for the solution that makes the audience remain to witness the play till the end, despite their knowledge of the biblical account. For there is always the possibility of the action of free will resulting in J. B.'s reaction different from that of Job in the Bible. It is the watching for such a possibility that creates suspense. The use of the biblical method establishes a supernatural plane for the beginning and the middle of the play, in which God is continually being addressed. What breaks the unity in the piece is the switching from the level of theology to that of humanism at the end, since the answer to the question, "Why does God make man suffer?" proposed at the beginning of the play descends to the humanistic plane exalting man for being able, through love, to bear suffering, regardless of its apparent meaninglessness.

J. B., to use Dr. Lucas' term, is a "simple" tragedy of circumstance, in which men are shown as the sport of invisible powers.[36] From this viewpoint, the play of MacLeish comes nearer to the narrow

---

[36] *Op. cit.*

sense of tragic as the "cosmic sense of the problem of evil, the mystery of the cruelty of things."[37] In this, despite its use of the biblical method of parataxis, *J. B.* is not biblical in spirit.

On the other hand, *L'Annonce faite à Marie* makes use of the plausibility of plot, the events being causally connected as advocated by exponents of classical drama. Instead of a chorus to give the exposition, Claudel dramatizes even the events of the past, presenting them in the Prologue. The lyrical role of the chorus is further supplied at intervals in the play by means of the ringing of the Angelus. If we study the plot in *L'Annonce,* we are impressed by the closely knit structure. An event that belongs to the past—Violaine's kiss for the leper, by means of which she had expressed acceptance of her role of suffering for the universe—is shown in its consequences in the events which make up the body of the drama. For this kiss which had been witnessed by Mara becomes the reason for her affliction with leprosy, of the alienation of Jacques from her, and of her nearness to God in her suffering, which prompts Mara to have recourse to her later. The suffering of Violaine, on the other hand, makes her godlike in pardon while rendering her so intensely human as to be able to enter into the interests of others. And this suffering, which is a re-enactment of the redemptive act of Christ, results in the salvation of others.

While *L'Annonce* follows the rule of causal probability, it does not disregard the biblical method. For although each event is shown in its relation to the others, the totality of the design which these events form is likewise unfolded in its relation to God.

If *J. B.* is a "simple" tragedy of circumstance, we may call *L'Annonce faite à Marie* a "complex" tragedy of recoil [38] showing events in their causal interrelatedness. Seen from the point of view of Jacques and Mara, *L'Annonce* is a tragedy with a plot enriched by a peripeteia and anagnorisis. On account of Jacques' loathing for Violaine's leprosy, which he associates with leprosy of soul, he, so to speak, cooperates with events leading to her being thrown out of her home. On the other hand, Mara, obsessed with the idea of winning Jacques for her husband, succeeds in her plan of making her mother persuade Violaine to give him up. The subsequent events lead to the anagnorisis at the end of the play when Jacques receives the astound-

---

37 Cf. pp. 77-78 of this book.
38 Lucas, *op. cit.,* p. 100.

ing revelation that Violaine, whom he has suspected of infidelity, is in fact innocent; that she has loved him, that despite betrayal she has pardoned Mara, that it is Violaine who has given life back to Mara's child. For Mara and Jacques, the full peripeteia has been completed: in working to win Jacques' love which she thought would bring her happiness, Mara has brought on herself the contempt of Jacques. He, on the other hand, in thinking of punishing Violaine by abandoning her, has brought about his own punishment in a life to be led with Mara whose worthlessness and despicableness he has at last discovered.

The plot involves intense conflict, both on the part of Jacques and Mara, and on the part of Violaine. In Mara, there is the struggle to keep Jacques' love even if she has to betray her own sister; there is in her a persistent effort to keep Jacques' affection for herself. In Jacques, there is the agony of the perpetual remembrance of the goodness he has known in Violaine, of doubt and suspicion regarding her real self. There is, moreover, the conflict resulting in the decision to accept the tragedy of life anew, with all its grimness. On the part of Violaine, there is the unfathomable sorrow of one who has been abandoned, of one who has had the promise of love but not its fulfillment. From the human point of view, her life is a tragedy, but in Claudel's drama, it is a triumph of love—love stronger than hate, love stronger than death, love that is the pledge of a resurrection. It is the Christian view which pervades this play with its plot modeled after the "beautifully forged chain of causation," true to the classical tradition of Greek drama. The ringing of Easter bells is a forecast of triumph similar to Christ's Resurrection, a triumph which is not a part of the action being presented in the drama, but an anticipated future giving the tragic events their meaning.

From ancient times, there has been a divided opinion regarding the tragic character. According to Aristotle, he must be good, that is to say, noble. He should, moreover, be appropriate or true to type, and consistent or true to himself. The Aristotelian tragic hero falls, not through sheer wickedness but through some flaw (hamartia) or through an act of overbearing self-sufficiency that calls down the wrath of the gods on him (hubris).

Even in ancient Greece, however, Euripides' characters did not fall under Aristotle's classification of tragic character. For in the Aristotelian theory of character, tragedy must present men as better than they are in daily life. Euripides, on the other hand, presented men as they were in life.

In recent times, there has been a tendency to present men as worse than they are in real life, to put "low men on a totem pole."[39]

The conditions of the age, the dramatist's vision, as well as the demands of the audience, among other things, affect the selection of the tragic character. But one thing seems to be true at all times: whether presented as finer than men ordinarily are, the tragic character must suffer and be taken seriously in his suffering. Because drama is an art, and art is necessarily selective, the dramatist will have a reason for presenting a certain character rather than another; there must be something in him worth treating seriously, exciting pity, if not admiration, something that rouses reflection rather than laughter.

In MacLeish's drama, the characters are noteworthy from the point of view of wealth and social position. Moreover, there are, in J. B., qualities that warrant MacLeish's choice of him as a tragic character: the tenacity of J. B.'s Puritan belief in God, his steadfastness to what he thinks his duty. In Sarah, too, at the beginning, there is gratitude to God and the desire to train her children in this gratitude.

As the drama unfolds, however, and the misfortunes are shown as occurring in succession, J. B. shows imaginative barrenness, not to speak of spiritual. One can say that his reaction to the trials sent by God is a sort of mechanical repetition of the words pronounced by his biblical counterpart: "The Lord has given, the Lord has taken; blessed be the name of the Lord." J. B. is devoid of the flights of poetic imagination which make the speech of Job in the Book of Books sublime. Neither does he have the soul-stirring faith of the man of God whose spirit can behold, if it cannot fathom, the depths of the wisdom of God. If we look for hamartia in this New England banker, shall we not find it in this barrenness of imagination, of emotion and of faith?

On the part of Sarah, hamartia can be seen in the sentimentality taking the place of love. This wife of a prosperous New England banker could be grateful in prosperity, faithful to J. B. when all went well, but unfaithful to him in illness and disaster. The heart that could not be moved to compassion on seeing her life companion afflicted with blisters from head to sole could be touched by the freshness

---

[39] John Gassner: *Theatre at the Crossroads* (New York: Holt, Rinehart and Winston, 1960), p. 158.

of the flower she had found blooming among the ashes in the ruins. There is hubris in Sarah's assertion that their prosperity has been the reward to their right living, and in the refusal to believe that God could allow misfortune to happen to them who are so righteous in life.

The catastrophe in this play is in itself hubris. For the greatest misfortune befalling J. B. and Sarah, from the Christian point of view, does not consist in the death of their children nor in the loss of their wealth, but in the hollowness of their faith. For, as the Scriptures have it, faith without charity is worthless.[40] And he who does not love God no longer really believes in Him. In declaring God to be merely existence without goodness and without love for His creatures, J. B. and Sarah are turning their backs on that Christianity which they profess externally at the opening of the play. Their faith has the flimsiness of a house built on sand: and when the wind and the rains came, that house fell because it was not built on solid ground.[41] J. B. and Sarah's turning their back on God and looking into themselves for the means to overcome suffering, from the Christian point of view, is smugness, a self-sufficiency which is toned down only by the hope expressed in the final lines: "to see by and by," probably the meaning of human suffering.

If we study MacLeish's characterization of J. B. and Sarah to see whether they are "appropriate" or "consistent," whether they are typical or individual, we find that they are types rather than individuals.[42] J. B. is the typical wealthy man of today who thinks he believes in God as his ancestors did. MacLeish evidently sees him as a Puritan who tends to think of suffering as punishment of guilt.[43] The persistent asking for the cause of the punishments being meted out to him, instead of the prayerful insight into the unfathomable wisdom of God, can also be considered typical of the man who has had more to do with material than with cultural and spiritual values. The bold unexpected conclusion which J. B.'s final speech reveals is typical of

---

[40] ". . .and if I should have all faith, that I could remove mountains, and have not charity, I am nothing." (I Cor. XIII, 2).

[41] Cf. Luke VI, 49.

[42] Aristotle's *Poetics*, XV, 1-5: "Appropriate" meaning "true to type," and "consistent" meaning true to themselves as individuals. Cf. Lucas, *op. cit.*, p. 107.

[43] V.L. Parrington, *The Colonial Mind* (New York: Harcourt, Brace and Co., c. 1927).

the independent thought which has characterized Puritanism since the beginning of its implantation in the New World.[44]

Sarah, the pretty wife of a successful banker, apparently affectionate in times of prosperity, is fickle in adversity. She can be counted upon as a pleasant companion in good times, but disappears when the need of her aid is greatest, which is to say that her love barely surmounts the vicissitudes that come in life.

The J. B. that MacLeish has drawn is the character of the well-off man who suffers today, not the Job of the Old Testament. Sarah, on the other hand, has more kinship with her biblical counterpart, while possessing qualities to make her representative of the contemporary woman in her social position. That MacLeish has succeeded in making us see in this couple the image of the man and woman of today is proof of his power of universalization, although they may not be sufficiently alive to haunt the imagination and stir the emotions as the greatest characters in fiction do.

This can of course be explained as due to the method of epic theater employed by MacLeish. Since he is aiming not at emotional identification with the characters but at a *Verfrendung,* we are not supposed to feel any attachment to them. It is to MacLeish's credit, however, that he has been able to present the tragic figures of the man and woman of today as he sees them. This play can be taken as MacLeish's criticism of the modern Job's spiritual dumbness, his lack of deep faith, of intensity whether in suffering or in exaltation. J. B. is just "dumb." Can it not be likewise an expression of the hope that although modern men do not believe in a God who loves, they may once more start in the long road toward Him through their love for one another which is a sharing in His divine life?

The characters in *L'Annonce faite à Marie* naturally fall into two groups: those who are presented as people are in actual life: Jacques, Mara and the mother; and those who are depicted as finer than men generally are: Pierre de Craon in later life, Anne Vercors and Violaine.

Each of these characters abounds in the reality that demands serious treatment in tragedy. All, with the exception of Violaine (unless her acceptance of the human condition is considered inability

44 See Solomon Stoddard's "Concerning Ancestors," in Perry Miller's *The American Puritans* (New York: Doubleday Anchor Books, 1956), pp. 222-24.

to protect herself), are presented as having a tragic flaw. In Jacques, the flaw lies in his incapacity to appreciate the splendor of the spirit beyond matter. In Mara, it is passion refusing to be governed either by faith or by reason. It is the hamartia in Jacques and in Mara that leads to the betrayal of Violaine and the exposure of the lie on which their life has been built. Likewise, to a certain degree, the tragic flaws in Pierre de Craon and in Anne Vercors are partly responsible for the tragedy of Violaine's betrayal. For, had not Pierre shown a weakening in his vocation, Violaine would not have seen the need for giving him the kiss of compassion because of which she contracted leprosy, denying herself a natural life of blessings in a happy family. As for Anne Vercors, had he understood from the beginning that one does not need to go to foreign lands in order to do God's will, he would have stayed to do his duty at Combernon. Had he not yielded to that wanderlust which brought him far from France, his daughter would not have been cast out of his home. Had it not been for the mother's mediocrity, she would have been able to convince Mara of her proper place, so that the tragic happenings in the family would have been avoided. Thus, we see that all the five characters, each with a tragic flaw, are fit for treatment even in drama without a biblical theme. Of all the characters in this play, however, Violaine is the most biblical. Her life best resembles the greatest tragic figure in the Christian world, the only tragic hero in Christianity beside whom all others are analogues: Christ. Like Mary's, Violaine's life was in perfect correspondence with the will of God. In this play, she symbolizes eternity invading time, living in time as though only one thing matters: the eternal. In the person of Violaine as the suffering victim, humanity rises from the "sphere below" to the "sphere beyond" to conciliate the divine.[45]

Yet, symbol though Violaine is, and typical of the biblical heroine as she is, she does not remain a mere symbol nor a mere type. She is a deeply human figure who can love intensely both those of her family and those who are related to her supernaturally; she finds it difficult to give up her fiancé, and she weakens in the moment when she is being abandoned by the people who should have protected her. But the supernatural triumphs over the natural in her, by her correspondence with grace. In her role of redemptive suffering, Violaine

---

[45] Balthasar, *loc. cit.*

becomes the center of the play, giving all the other events a place in the whole design of Providence in life. By her presence in the play, the world of the supernatural to which she belongs, and the realm of the earthly of which Mara and Jacques are a part, meet at the incident of Christmas, the day that celebrates the mystery of the divine taking on the form of humanity. And yet, supernatural as she is, she does not consider the things of the earth as beneath her. Her language is not aloof, she can meet people on their own ground. In her conversation with Pierre de Craon in the Prologue, she proves herself capable of satirical speech and pointed wit like any intelligent French woman. When Pierre de Craon, intending to give her the highest compliment, says, "Image of eternal beauty, you are not mine," she retorts, "I am not an image. That is no way to talk." Yet, as Pierre resumes, "in taking you, another man takes what was mine," Violaine replies with his own terminology: "You still have the image."[46] She can indeed seem to be a bundle of contradictions, and there is no saying how she can catch a man with his own words. She waives Pierre's sentimentality with the characteristic humor of the French peasant by indicating their different paths in life, referring to his life lived in steeples, thus:

> Well! We couldn't have set up housekeeping together. I cannot go up the hay-loft without getting dizzy.[47]

Like Violaine, the other characters in the play are typical as well as highly individual. Much as Jacques is typical of the peasant bound to the earth, he is nonetheless Jacques Hury, the fiancé very much in love with Violaine, resenting the rivalry which he suspects in Pierre de Craon, incapable of understanding supernatural motives, consoling himself with the substitute offered to him in the person of Mara, yet ever haunted by the very spiritual beauty in Violaine which he has not been able to comprehend. Mara, the jealous sister and passionate

---

[46] Fowlie's translation. In the original:
  Pierre: O image de la Beauté éternelle, tu n'es pas à moi!
  Violaine: Je ne suis pas une image! ce n'est pas une manière de dire les choses!
  Pierre: Un autre prend en vous ce qui était à moi.
  Violaine. Il reste l'image.
        (*Theatre II*, p. 143)
[47] Fowlie's translation. In the original:
  Eh bien! Nous n'aurions pas fait ménage ensemble!
  Je ne puis monter au grenier sans que la tête me tourne.
  (*Theatre II*, p. 144)

woman, is the peasant girl who finds ruses to get what she wants. She is Mara, the bitter one, keenly sensitive to her rights. Pierre de Craon is not merely a builder of churches living apart in steeples, but also a man of flesh and blood, moved to tenderness as well as to violence by the presence of a beautiful woman. The mother may be mediocre, but she has the nerve to contradict her husband, she knows his ways, and feels when tears alone can move him. Anne Vercors, for all his spiritual insight, has the natural tendencies of a father who favors his graceful, sympathetic daughter, and shows aloofness from the daughter who is lacking in the graces of a woman.

The personages in Claudel's drama then are, as Aristotle has said of the tragic characters, both "appropriate" or true to type, and "consistent" or true to themselves. In the Vercors family, there is the intensity which makes for tragic presentation. For in the passionate adherence to values, both natural and supernatural, the seeds of tragedy may be found. In *L'Annonce*, the passionate attachment to the things of the earth found in Mara and Jacques is bound to come into violent conflict with the equally ardent struggle to attain the supernatural, as found in Violaine, Anne Vercors and Pierre de Craon. The criticism which MacLeish has made of J. B.'s acting cannot be made of Claudel's characters:

> . . . goddam sheep
> Without the spunk to spit on Christmas.

Mara was the kind who would have the "spunk to spit" on anything.

As Dr. Lucas has said, ". . . not wickedness, but weakness remains the hardest of all human qualities to make dramatic;"[48] which reminds us of the lines from the Bible: "I know thy works, that thou art neither cold nor hot. I would thou wert cold or hot. But because thou art lukewarm and neither cold nor hot, I will begin to vomit thee out of my mouth."[49] An audience will find the dramatic in a scene characterized either by white-heat goodness or by wickedness capable of stupefying. And these we find in Claudel's drama.

* * *

The choice of a biblical theme for dramatic portrayal would, therefore, seem in no way to hinder tragic presentation. What deter-

---

[48] *Op. cit.*, p. 110.
[49] *Apocalypse*, III, 15-16.

mines the tragic quality of a play will be the intensity with which the dramatist presents some phase of human life. And the profundity of the faith of personages of the Bible can aid rather than hamper the dramatist in the construction of tragedy.

In both *J. B.* and *L'Annonce,* the dramatists have succeeded in varying degrees toward accomplishing what they aimed to present: Claudel's characters living the strength of faith when Christianity was life; MacLeish's plodding in a milieu where a struggling humanism may be replacing Christianity.

THE TERM BIBLICAL DRAMA

The possibility of treating the biblical theme in both comic and tragic veins has been studied; it has been shown how comedy can be enriched by biblical dimensions, and in what sense one can be justified in speaking of biblical tragedy. At the end of this study, it now seems pertinent to consider whether the modern plays that employ a biblical theme can be classified as biblical drama.

When speaking of biblical drama, one obviously means the dramatization of scriptural narrative, which is faithful to the content and the spirit of the original. Hence, in the previous discussions, I have kept away from the so-called pseudobiblical material in which association with Holy Scripture is but remote, consisting merely of setting or of incidents relating to characters but slightly connected with scriptural figures. Such, for example, are dramas devoted to Herod and Marianne, or to the fall of Jerusalem.

The mystery plays of the fifteenth and sixteenth centuries, as well as those in the succeeding periods during which the process of humanization had crept in, can be called biblical dramas without any reservation. The authorship of the mystery plays is generally unknown But they were, so to speak, almost literal renderings of Scripture. When poets of note, like Milton, started dramatizing scriptural material using a method which Murray Roston terms "postfigurative identification,"[50] the resulting play was still biblical drama with an added personal dimension. For in *Samson Agonistes,* in portraying the biblical hero, Milton was also projecting himself, identifying himself

---

[50] *Op. cit.,* p. 171.

with Samson in feelings and experiences, so that this biblical hero becomes an archetype "postfigured" by the Puritan poet who lived centuries later.

In the following age, Dryden's use of biblical parallels is motivated by a "desire to win applause for his wit and learning,"[51] distracting attention from scriptural subject matter, which is considered "rarely more than a vehicle for that wit." In his play *The State of Innocence and Fall of Man* (1677), there is too much "frigidity and intellectual word-play" to enable it to have serious grasp of character, there being "no attempt to revitalize the significance of scriptural events."[52] While Dryden makes use of biblical subject matter, his treatment of it leads to a departure into ways foreign to the spirit of Scripture. This departure becomes more and more noticeable in the nineteenth century as well as in the twentieth.

Among the plays studied in this work, Christopher Fry's *The Firstborn*, Archibald MacLeish's *Nobodaddy*, Marc Connelly's *The Green Pastures* and Andre Obey's *Noah* employ the postfigurative identification found in Milton's drama; but the parallels have broadened from personal to social or political dimensions. Instead of identification of the author with the hero in *The Firstborn*, there are parallels between the modern dictator and the Pharaoh, Seti; in *Nobodaddy*, the parallel is between Adam and the twentieth-century technician who wishes to build a world apart from and surpassing God's own world; in *The Green Pastures*, there is a projection of a naive Negro society; in *Noah*, the playwright portrays the predicament of the modern family through a presentation of the patriarch's. Yet, for all these varieties in the reading of Scripture, the above-mentioned plays may still be classified as biblical dramas with modern undertones. The essentials of the biblical narrative remain; the scriptural content and spirit have not been changed, but are merely viewed with the eyes of a modern author aware of various parallels between his world and the world of the biblical heroes.

It is in Giraudoux's *Judith* that the undertones are not merely nonbiblical but also antibiblical. The subject matter is rather the "fille-a-la-mode" in the guise of Judith but worlds apart from this heroine in her spirit. However, startling though this play is in exegesis

---

51 *Ibid.*, p. 178.
52 *Ibid.*, p. 179.

and in character portrayal, *Judith* is still a dramatization of the apocryphal narrative with an interpretation that is decidedly anti-biblical; hence the hesitation in classifying this play as biblical drama.

From Shaw's *Back to Methuselah* through O'Neill's *Lazarus Laughed,* there is an even greater freedom in the handling of biblical themes. Each of these plays starts with a biblical situation. In the Shaw play, the point of departure is the situation of Adam and Eve in Eden. But from this, the dramatist shoots, so to speak, into free space, with imagined events of the future for plot, illustrating his theory of creative evolution. On the other hand, O'Neill takes the incident of Lazarus rising from the dead as a starting point in the illustration of the theory of eternal recurrence. Evidently, the scriptural material in both of these plays is too meager to justify our calling them biblical dramas, the fictional part being overwhelmingly dominant. Still, the playwrights at least commence with a dramatization of biblical motifs.

In the rest of the plays discussed in this study, there is a drastic change in the content and dramaturgy. In these plays, it seems to me, modern drama has come into its own in the handling of biblical themes. In *J. B.* as in *L'Annonce faite à Marie, Murder in the Cathedral, Cantique de Cantiques* and in *A Sleep of Prisoners,* what is being dramatized is no longer the biblical narrative. It is an embellished historical event, or some imagined sequence of events in life, past or contemporary, given unparalleled dimensions by the deliberate provision of biblical undertones. Whereas in the plays of Milton and Dryden, and even in those of Christopher Fry, MacLeish, Connelly and Obey previously studied, the events and characters were obviously biblical but with secular undertones, in the distinctively modern dramas employing biblical themes, it is vice versa: the plot and characters are not drawn from Scripture; only the undertones are scriptural.

To one ignorant of the Bible, the action in these plays possesses a meaning of its own, but the full message can be grasped only by one who is aware of the scriptural implications. Here we have drama fully grown and metamorphosed from the seeds sown in the form of mystery plays that delighted audiences three or four centuries ago. But such drama which our modern playwrights are producing in employing scriptural themes can no longer be classified as biblical drama. They are not the dramatizations of scriptural material that used to entertain medieval audiences. For, needless to say, today's audiences would be bored with a mere dramatization of Scripture. They have even become immune to the shock of the naturalistic exegesis of biblical material. And so, the dramatists have found the means of approaching these audiences, reaching depths which they could not otherwise fathom, stirring in their subconscious memories of the Scripture which form part of their cultural heritage.

When modern drama employs the scriptural theme, therefore, more often than not, the outcome is no longer biblical drama, the biblical being recognizable only in the undertones.

CHAPTER SIX

Structural Metamorphosis
in Dramatic Art—Biblical Themes
as Mythopoeic Designs

In his essay on "The Theory of Myths,"[1] Northrop Frye declares that "The possession of originality cannot make an artist unconventional; it drives him further into convention, obeying the law of art itself, which seeks constantly to reshape itself from its own depths, and which works through its geniuses for metamorphosis, as it works through minor talents for mutation."

As has been noted earlier in this work, the efforts of playwrights in our century have been characterized by a struggle for innovation. There is something outmoded in old theories of dramatic art, and playwrights are groping for newer methods of expressing the life in their age.

In studying a number of playwrights who employ the biblical theme, I have become strongly aware of this varied search for new techniques in drama. However, it is paradoxical to say that in their search for ways of innovation, playwrights actually strike at the very roots of their cultural tradition—the biblical heritage.

The employment of the biblical theme may have sprung from religious fervor, as in the case of Paul Claudel, of Christopher Fry and T.S. Eliot. But whether the dramatists taken up in this study approve the biblical message or question it, one thing remains true— each of them has been trying to use the biblical theme as a structural design for dramatic literature that possesses relevance to our times.

---

[1] Northrop Frye, *Anatomy of Criticism* (New York: Atheneum, 1969), p. 132.

The development of MacLeish's dramatic treatment of the biblical theme serves to illustrate the trend in the dramatic literature that has adopted biblical themes for structural organization. His *Nobodaddy* (1925) hardly differs from the mystery plays except in minor points. For in *Nobodaddy*, it is the happenings before and after the Fall of Man which are being dramatized, despite the lifelikeness in the psychological presentation of the characters which makes them remind us of the people around us today. In *J. B.,* written after a lapse of three decades, MacLeish dramatizes present-day life. Witnessing this play, however, one becomes greatly aware of its use of the biblical pattern of the *Book of Job*. The incidents in *J. B.* are realistic enough to be plausible, yet it is not these happenings which hold the interest of the audience, but rather the structural design which gives shape to the play. The literary shape grows before the mind's eye of the audience, and as it does, watching it, people are aware of a movement on two levels: the contemporary and the biblical. And as the audience sit back, they wait for the culmination of the play which will show them how the dramatist has utilized these two levels to bring about a harmonious piece of art. To the devices used in solving the problem of making realistic fiction plausible while at the same time employing some structural design, Northrop Frye has given the term "displacement."[2] The events comprising the plot of the biblical archetype have been displaced by events occurring in our times. The characters are those whom we see in our modern society. And yet, their acts and words call forth associations with the biblical characters who are their counterparts. The total impression made by such a literary piece is that of complexity: a high degree of stylization which is the direction toward which the dramatists experimenting on the handling of the biblical theme as studied in this work are seen to tend.

In the first group of plays studied in the section entitled "Re-creation of Biblical Characters through Psychology," despite the apparent fidelity to the original version of the Bible, only two plays, *The Firstborn* and *Nobodaddy,* have the biblical theme undisplaced. Mainly it is the biblical story that Christopher Fry dramatizes and it is the biblical characters whom he delineates in *The Firstborn*. Such is the case, too, in MacLeish's *Nobodaddy*. In the next three plays

---

[2] *Ibid.,* p. 136.

studied, a certain degree of displacement has occurred: in Giraudoux's play, the heroine of the Old Testament has given way to Judith, the *fille-a-la-mode*; in Connelly's *The Green Pastures,* the Louisiana Negroes have taken the place of the biblical characters, whereas in Andre Obey's *Noah,* the family that enters, lives in and departs from the ark is evidently the family of today with its problems.

If we reconsider the other plays treated in this work, we shall realize that the displacements increase in accordance with the degree of stylization undertaken by the dramatist. Beyond the stylization achieved by Christopher Fry in *A Sleep of Prisoners*, it is probably difficult to proceed. In this play with its complexity of thematic design, the movement toward stylization in dramatic art must have reached the extreme side of reaction to the representational lifelikeness of naturalism on the stage.

That the stylization in dramatic literature achieved through the displacements effected in the use of biblical themes in structural organization is only a part in a greater movement in the fictional literature of our age, we have the words of Eliot previously quoted. Commenting on the method followed in *Ulysses*, the poet-critic claimed that in using the mythical method, James Joyce was taking a method which others would pursue after him.[3] T.S. Eliot was then thinking of Greek myth, such as he himself later used in structuring his dramas. Even more evident is the use of Greek myth as pattern for plot and characters in Eugene O'Neill's trilogy, *Mourning Becomes Electra*. Instead of the Greek background, in the O'Neill play we have the post-Civil War New England. The main characters in the *Oresteia* trilogy of Aeschylus all have their counterparts in the O'Neill play: General Ezra Mannon comes back to his home where his wife Christine has had an affair with a Captain Adam Brunt. Upon the general's return, his quarrel with his wife is understandable; so is his being stricken with heart attack, during which Christine substitutes poison for his medicine, thus murdering him. In line with the Oresteian story, the subsequent revenge undertaken by the son, Orin, and the daughter, Lavinia, leads to the murder of Captain Brunt and the suicide of their unfaithful mother. Tragedy haunts brother and sister in their perverted relationship, ending with Orin's suicide and Lavinia's retirement into

---

[3] Cf. p. 37 of this book.

the gloomy Mannon home where she is to spend her remaining days with the ghosts of her family's past.

It is significant that O'Neill experimented with the integration of biblical and Greek themes respectively to provide structure for his dramas: *Lazarus Laughed* in 1926 and *Mourning Becomes Electra* in 1931. In both, it is the mythical method that is employed: the use of primeval events provided by the biblical and Greek traditions as patterns for events happening in another age.

One might question, however, the term "mythical method" employed in connection with the use of biblical themes; hence the necessity of considering the term "myth" at this juncture. Myth has so often been associated with the fictions, the half-truths forming part of the ideology of society, that there is a certain hesitation in using this term in connection with the Bible. However, the term "myth" has come to be used to denote "any recurring theme or character type that appeals to the consciousness of a people by embodying its cultural ideals or by giving expression to deep, commonly felt emotions."[4] In his book, *Patterns in Comparative Religion,* Mircea Eliade claims that "every myth expresses a new cosmic 'situation' or primeval event which becomes, simply by being expressed, a paradigm for all time to come."[5] As such, the myth, in recounting an event that occurred *in illo tempore*, becomes, so to speak, "a precedent and a pattern for all the actions and 'situations' later to repeat that event."[6] Elsewhere, Eliade speaks of the majority of myths as constituting an "exemplar history which can be repeated, and whose meaning and value lie in that very repetition."[7] According to this point of view, the expression of primeval events taking place *in illo tempore* of the biblical world can be validly called myth. Hence, the integration of biblical themes in the structural organization of plays may be termed mythical method.

The impulse that made dramatists use the biblical theme in plays considered in this paper seems to me to be a movement resulting in a structural metamorphosis in the dramatic art of our century. When the Greek dramatists wrote their plays, what they were presenting to

---

[4] Definition 3 given by *The American Heritage Dictionary of the English Language.*
[5] Mircea Eliade, *Patterns in Comparative Religion* (New York: The World Publishing Co., 1963), p. 416.
[6] *Ibid.,* p. 429.
[7] *Ibid.,* p. 430.

the audience was just what the actors were performing on the stage. Witnessing the representation of the life of gods and heroes, the audience could, through emotional identification, imagine the same situations and events as applying to themselves. On the other hand, the structure in the plays using the biblical theme according to the mythical method is such that while characters in the present or in some period in history are delineated as talking and acting, we are aware of something other than their words and acts—we have an association of characters talking and acting farther back in the past of the biblical narrative. The result of the witnessing of such a play is a certain consciousness of the continuity of patterns in life: the archetypes in the biblical tradition are visible in the structure of the life in our times as well as in other ages. The conclusion which an audience witnessing a play with the mythical method arrives at is oblique as compared with that in the representational method which is direct. This may be illustrated by the following diagrams:

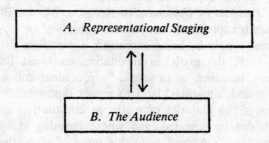

Figure 1

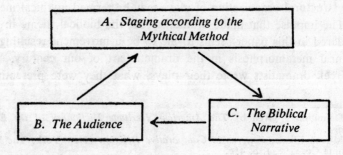

Figure 2

As shown in Figure 1, the audience attending a play according to the representational staging takes in directly what is being said and acted. In Figure 2, however, the perception of the meaning of the play becomes oblique. In witnessing the staging of a play written in the mythical method, the audience's perception reaches beyond the words and acts of the personages to those of the personages in the biblical narrative in which the pattern for the play is recognizable.

The use of the mythical method in the integration of a biblical theme within the structure of drama, as has been seen, thus enhances the freedom of the playwright. The awareness of the biblical structure is noticeable even in plays like *Judith* and *Cantique de Cantiques* which are colored by parody, or in *The Green Pastures* where humor is predominant. The use of the biblical theme, therefore, is not a limiting device, but rather a means of giving freedom to the dramatist by enabling him to enlarge the dimensions of his poetic vision of life through the transparency of mythopoeic designs integrating the fragmented events in the life of another age. Depending on whether the dramatist's vision is of the exalted or the ironic, the language of the play will vary.

This awareness of the biblical theme which has taken hold of certain dramatists in their presentation of life on the stage is but an expression of what T.S. Eliot has termed the "historical sense" involving "a perception, not only of the pastness of the past, but of its presence."[8] In writing his play, the dramatist "lives in what is not merely present but the present moment of the past,"[9] conscious that in the events of his own times as well as in other periods of history, the biblical archetypes continue rising into life. This perception of the oneness of the past and the present is an activity of reason that tends to unify reality, reducing "the multiplicity of things to a single 'situation' "[10] found in the biblical archetype. In this process, the fragmented events of the past and of the present come to reveal a basic oneness with a pattern seen in primeval events as expressed in the biblical narrative. Thus, in recognizing a similar pattern in the isolated events of life, the contemporary dramatist, a representative of modern men, discovers himself and is able to understand himself

---

8 "Tradition and the Individual Talent," *Selected Essays,* p. 14.
9 *Ibid.,* p. 22.
10 Eliade, *op. cit.,* p. 453.

because these designs in Scripture "express cosmic realities which ultimately he is aware of as realities in his own being."[11]

What we have seen in this study as true regarding the drama, T.S. Eliot had already noticed as true regarding the novel at the time he commented on James Joyce's *Ulysses*. The use of the biblical theme in modern drama, resulting in structural metamorphosis in the art through what Eliot calls the mythical method, is, therefore, but a part in a great movement in the literature of our century which through its geniuses is constantly seeking "to reshape itself from its own depths"—indeed from the very roots of its traditions.

---

[11] *Ibid.*, p. 456.

Bibliography

Auerbach, Erich. *Scenes from the Drama of European Literature: Six Essays*. New York: Meridian, 1959.

————————. *Mimesis: The Representation of Reality in Western Literature,* trans. Willard Trask. New York: Doubleday & Co., 1957.

Aylen, Leo. *Greek Tragedy and the Modern World*. London: Methuen & Co., 1964.

Balthasar, Hans Urs von. "Das Tragische und der Christliche Glaube," *Hochland,* LVII (August 1965).

Bentley, Eric. *The Life of the Drama*. New York: Atheneum, 1965.

————————. *The Playwright as Thinker*. New York: The World Publishing Co., c. 1946.

Berrigan, Daniel. "A Play that Failed," *America,* October 4, 1958.

Bradbrook, M.C. *English Dramatic Form: A History of Its Development*. London: Chatto & Windus, 1965.

Brecht, Bertolt. *Plays,* Vol. 2: "Mother Courage and Her Children" trans. Eric Bentley, "St. Joan of the Stockyards" trans. Frank Jones, "The Good Person of Szechwan" trans. John Willet. London: Methuen & Co., 1962.

Brooks, Cleanth (ed.). *Tragic Themes in Western Literature*. New Haven: Yale University Press, c. 1955.

Browne, E. Martin (ed.). *Religious Drama 2: Mystery and Morality Plays*. New York: Meridian Books, 1959.

Broussard, Louis. *American Drama: Contemporary Allegory from Eugene O'Neill to Tennessee Williams*. Norman: University of Oklahoma Press, 1962.

Bush, Warren V. *The Dialogues of Archibald MacLeish and Mark Van Doren*. New York: E.P. Dutton & Co., 1964.

Cazamian, L. *A History of French Literature.* Oxford: Clarendon Press, 1955.

Chaigne, Louis. *La Vie de Paul Claudel et genese de son oeuvre.* France: Maison Mame, 1961.

Clark, Barrett H. (ed.) *European Theories of the Drama.* New York: Crown Publishers, 1965.

Claudel, Paul. *Theatre de Paul Claudel* I. Librairie Gallimard, 1956.

*——————. *Theatre de Paul Claudel* II. Librairie Gallimard, 1956.

——————. *L'Annonce faite à Marie.* Librairie Gallimard, 1940.

——————. *Oeuvre Poetique.* Librairie Gallimard, 1957.

——————. *The Tidings Brought to Mary,* trans. Wallace Fowlie. Chicago: Henry Regnery Co., 1960.

——————. *The Satin Slipper,* trans. John O'Connor. New York: Sheed and Ward.

*Connelly, Marc. "The Green Pastures," *Twentieth Century Plays: American.* Ed. Richard Cordell. New York: The Ronald Press Co., c. 1947.

Dahlstrom, Carl Enoch William Leonard. *Strindberg's Dramatic Expressionism.* Ann Arbor: University of Michigan, 1930.

Driver, Tom F. "Clean Miss," *The Christian Century,* June 11, 1958.

Eliade, Mircea. *Patterns in Comparative Religion.* New York: The World Publishing Co., 1963.

Eliot, T.S. *Collected Plays.* London: Faber and Faber Ltd., 1962.

——————. *The Family Reunion.* London: Faber and Faber Ltd., 9th impression, 1956.

*——————. *Murder in the Cathedral.* London: Faber and Faber Ltd., 1935.

——————. *Poetry and Drama.* London: Faber and Faber Ltd., 1951.

——————. *On Poetry and Poets.* New York: The Noonday Press, 1961.

——————. *Selected Essays.* London: Faber and Faber Ltd., 1963.

——————. "Ulysses, Order, and Myth," *Dial* LXXV (November 1923).

---

* Marked with an asterisk are titles of books that served as primary sources in the writing of this work.

————————. *The Use of Poetry and the Use of Criticism*. London: Faber and Faber Ltd., 1933.

Esslin, Martin. *Brecht: The Man and His Work*. New York: Doubleday & Co., Inc., 1960.

Feldman, Irving. "Job in Modern Dress," *Commentary,* August 1958.

Fergusson, Francis. *The Idea of a Theater*. Garden City: Doubleday & Co., 1953.

"First-Nighters Cheered," *Newsweek,* December 22, 1958.

Fowlie, Wallace. *Claudel*. London: Bowes & Bowes, 1957.

————————. *A Guide to Contemporary French Literature from Valery to Sartre*. New York: Meridian Books, c. 1957.

Frenzel, Elizabeth. *Stoffe der Weltliteratur*. Kroner, 1963.

Fry, Christopher. *The Boy with a Cart*. London: Oxford University Press, 1939.

————————. "Comedy," *The Tulane Drama Review,* IV, 3 (March 1960).

————————. *Curtmantle*. London: Oxford University Press, 1961.

*————————. *The Firstborn*. London: Oxford University Press, 1949.

*————————. *A Sleep of Prisoners*. London: Oxford University Press, 1951.

————————. *Thor with Angels*. London: Oxford University Press, 1949.

Frye, Northrop. *Anatomy of Criticism: Four Essays*. New York: Atheneum, 1969.

Garten, H.F. *Modern German Drama*. London: Methuen and Co., 1959.

Gascoigne, Bamber. *Twentieth Century Drama*. London: Hutchinson & Co., Ltd., 1962.

Gassner, John. *Form and Idea in Modern Theatre*. New York: The Dryden Press, 1956.

————————. (ed.). *Ideas in the Drama*. New York: Columbia University Press, 1964.

————————. *Theatre at the Crossroads*. New York: Holt, Rinehart and Winston, 1960.

* Giraudoux, Jean. *Cantique des Cantiques*. Paris: Bernard Grasset, c. 1939.

*————————. *Judith*. Paris: Grasset, 1932.

———————. "The Song of Songs," trans. John Raikes, *The Tulane Drama Review,* III, 4 (May 1959).

Gribben, John L. "Shaw's Saint Joan: A Tragic Heroine," *Thought,* XL, 59 (Winter, 1965).

Guicharnaud, James, and Junde Beckelman. *Modern French Theatre from Giraudoux to Beckett.* New Haven: Yale University Press, 1961.

Hebbel, F. "Maria Magdalena," trans. Barber Fairley. *Everyman's Library.* London: J.M. Dent.

Hewes, Henry. "A Minority Report on *J.B.,*" *Saturday Review,* January 3, 1959.

Holy Bible
   Douai-Rheims Version, with Bishop Challoner's Notes, Newly Compiled Indices, Tables and Verified References. London: Burns Oates and Washbourne, 1914.
   King James Version. New York: American Bible Society.
   Revised Standard Version, Catholic Edition. London: The Catholic Truth Society, 1966.
   The Jerusalem Bible. London: Geoffrey Chapman, 1971.

Howe, George, and Gustave Adolphus Harrer (eds.). *Greek Literature in Translation.* New York: Harper & Brothers, 1924.

"Job and J. B.," *Time,* December 22, 1958.

Julleville, Petit de. *Le Théâtre en France.* Paris: Librairie Armand Colin, 1923.

Karmann, Adolf D. "Friedrich Duerrenmatt and the Tragic Sense of Comedy," *The Tulane Drama Review,* IV, 4 (May 1960).

Krutch, Joseph Wood. *American Drama since 1918.* New York: George Braziller, Inc., 1957.

———————. "The Universe at Stage Center," *Theatre Arts,* August 1958.

Lucas, F.L. *Tragedy.* New York: Collier Books, c. 1957, 1962.

Lucy, Sean. *T.S. Eliot and the Idea of Tradition.* London: Cohen & West, 1967.

Lumley, Frederick. *Trends in 20th Century Drama.* London: Barrie and Rockliff, 1961.

MacLeish, Archibald. *Air Raid.* New York: Harcourt, Brace and Co., 1938.

———————. *The American Story.* New York: Duell, Sloan and Pearce, 1944.

—————————. *The Collected Poems of Archibald MacLeish*. Boston: Houghton Mifflin Co., 1962.

* —————————. *J. B.* Boston: Houghton Mifflin Co., 1961.

* —————————. *Nobodaddy*. Cambridge: Dunster House, 1926.

—————————. *Panic*. Boston: Houghton Mifflin Co. 1935.

—————————. *This Music Crept by Me upon the Waters*. Cambridge: Harvard University Press. 1953.

—————————. *A Time to Speak*. Boston: Houghton Mifflin Co., 1941.

—————————. *Poetry and Opinion*. University of Illinois Press, 1950.

—————————. *Poetry and Experience*. London: The Bodley Head, 1960.

Madaule, Jacques. *Le Drame de Paul Claudel*. Paris: Desclee de Brower et Cie, 1947.

Mason, Donald E. "The Disintegration of New England Puritanism," *Tradition and Creation,* ed. by J. Roggendorf, S.J. Tokyo: Sophia University, 1963.

Mason, H.S. "Existentialism and Literature," *Scrutiny*, XIII:1. Cambridge University Press, 1950–51.

Miller, Perry (ed.). *The American Puritans: Their Prose and Poetry*. New York: Doubleday Anchor Books, 1956.

Miller, Perry, and Thomas H. Johnson (eds.). *The Puritans, I*. New York: Harper & Row, 1963.

Milward, Peter. "The Base Judean," *Shakespeare Studies,* I. The Shakespeare Society of Japan, 1962.

Morison, Samuel Eliot. *The Intellectual Life of Colonial New England*. Ithaca: Cornell University Press, c. 1956.

Moulton, R.G. *The Literary Study of the Bible*. Boston: C.C. Heath & Co., 1899.

Murdock, Kenneth B. *Literature and Theology in Colonial New England*. Cambridge: Harvard University Press, 1949.

Nicoll, Allardyce. *British Drama*. London: George G. Harrap, 1961.

* Obey, Andre. *Noah*, trans. Arthur Wilmurt. New York: Samuel French, c. 1935.

O'Flaherty, Kathleen. *Paul Claudel and "The Tidings Brought to Mary."* Westminster, Maryland: The Newman Press, 1949.

* O'Neill, Eugene. "Lazarus Laughed," *Nine Plays*. New York: The Modern Library, c. 1954.

Parrington, Vernon L. *The Colonial Mind.* New York: Harcourt, Brace and Co., c. 1927.

"The Patience of Job," *Time,* March 24, 1958.

Racine, Jean Baptiste. *Théâtre complet.* Paris: Garnier Freres, 1960.

Richards, I.A. *Principles of Literary Criticism.* London: Routledge & Kegan Paul, Inc., 1952 (13th impression).

Roggendorf, J. "Review of Elizabeth Frenzel's 'Stoffe der Weltliteratur,'" *Sophia* (Winter, 1962).

Roston, Murray. *Biblical Drama in England: From the Middle Ages to the Present Day.* London: Faber and Faber, 1968.

* Shaw, Bernard. "Back to Methuselah," *The Complete Plays.* London: Constable and Co., 1931.

—————. *Major Critical Essays: 'The Quintessence of Ibsenism,' 'The Perfect Wagnerite,' 'The Sanity of Art.'* London: Constable and Co., 1955 reprint.

Smith, Carol D. *T.S. Eliot's Dramatic Theory and Practice.* Princeton: Princeton University Press, 1963.

Stanford, Derek. *Christopher Fry, An Appreciation.* London: Peter Nevill Ltd., 1951.

Stuart, Donald Clive. *The Development of Dramatic Art.* New York: Dover Publications, 1960.

"Three Opinions on *J. B.,*" *Life,* June 22, 1959.

Trawick, Buckner B. *The Bible as Literature: Old Testament History and Biography.* New York: Barnes & Noble, c. 1963.

Tynan, Kenneth. "The Theatre: Portrait of the Artist as a Young Camera," *The New Yorker,* December 20, 1958.

Vachon, Andre. *Le Temps et L'espace dans l'oeuvre de Paul Claudel.* Editions du Seuil, 1965.

Wilder, Thornton. *Three Plays.* New York: Bantam Books, 1961.

—————. *'The Long Christmas Dinner' and Other Plays in One Act.* New York: Harper & Row, c. 1963.

Willet, John. *The Theatre of Bertolt Brecht.* London: Methuen & Co., 1960.

Wood, Michael. "A Study of Fire Imagery in Some Plays by Paul Claudel," *French Studies,* April 1965.

Index